MW00333705

THE NEW ART OF
RAISING
HAPPY
KIDS

CENTENNIAL BOOKS

CENTENNIAL BOOKS

THE NEW ART OF

RAISING

HAPPY

KIDS

**How to Navigate Social Media,
Bullying, Nutrition, Sleep
& Effective Communication**

BY ALYSSA SHAFFER

58

Chapter 1

CREATING STRONG BONDS

Chapter 2

KEEPING KIDS HEALTHY

Chapter 3

GROWTH AND DEVELOPMENT

Chapter 4

NAVIGATING THE WORLD AT LARGE

Creating Strong Bonds

Follow these essential parenting tips to help your children stay happy and secure at every age.

Help for Raising Happy Kids

We all want our kids to grow up being joyful.
Here's what parenting experts recommend
we do to raise a well-adjusted, confident child.

1 Step Back to Problem-Solve

Too often, parenting tends to be reactive, says Ari S. Yares, PhD, a licensed psychologist based in Potomac, Maryland. "But you have to be willing to engage in new ideas, and it's difficult to do that when you're in a survivor mindset." For example, take packing up school lunches: At Yares' house, he found he was spending what felt like half the night getting lunches prepared for six people–and much of the time, those lunches were coming back home, half-eaten. So he sat down with his kids and explained that his time was valuable and needed to be used for the things only he could do–which meant his kids needed to get in on the lunch-making process. "We tried it, and it was a disaster–the meals were totally unbalanced; the kids were late getting to school, because they were packing up in the morning; and they still weren't eating what they packed." So they went back to square one and had a brainstorming session. "We had a conversation about healthier eating choices, figured out what they wanted to eat, came up with a shopping list and made sure we had what they needed on hand. And after that, we definitely saw an improvement, even if it was just an incremental one."

The idea behind innovative parenting, says Yares, is to start by observing and asking questions, then figuring out strategies that work. "Ask yourself, what are the principles and values that are important to you, and then what you can do to solve whatever problems or issues you may face." You have to be willing to experiment, he adds, and–as with the lunch process–you probably will have setbacks; but "if you fail and try again, it will ultimately make for healthier parenting."

2 Emphasize Both Rules and Relationships

"Rules without relationships can lead to rebellion," notes Joy Acaso, LCSW, a psychotherapist and parent-child relationship specialist in Fort Lauderdale, Florida. On the other hand, she notes, "you can't have relationships without structure or boundaries." That means making sure your child gets her homework done on time, but also praising her for her hard work. "You have to have a synergy of both to make the most impact," says Acaso.

The first rule of happiness? Create a warm and fostering environment for your kids.

✕

Research shows that our brain is hardwired to do one task at a time, not several. So forget multitasking—give your kids all your attention when you can.

3 Maintain High Standards and Low Expectations

Parents naturally want their kids to get straight As or excel at particular sports or activities; but more often than not, they'll get cut from the team or earn a disappointing grade on an exam. "Don't become disgruntled or get upset. Things aren't always going to go as planned, so our job is to stay calm and help kids learn, if and when they fail," says John Mayer, PhD, a clinical psychologist and parenting consultant based in Chicago. Kids learn resilience, just like other life skills; the more you can help them try again, the more success they will ultimately have.

4 Offer Less

We're often so busy trying to give our kids everything they may need that we don't realize we're simply overloading them, notes Natasha Beck, PsyD, a clinical psychologist based in Los Angeles. "Having too many games, gadgets and other toys can get overwhelming." If you give your child one of 10 books to choose from instead of trying to pick from dozens, it can help him focus and feel less frustrated. "Try to simplify things as much as you can—it doesn't make you less of a parent to give fewer choices," she adds.

5 Check in With Your Kids— Every Day

"These days, kids too often fly under the radar. They may be depressed, anxious, angry, scared—and they think you're too busy to talk to them about it, or not interested, so they don't make an effort to tell you," observes Carole Lieberman, MD, a child psychiatrist based in Beverly Hills, California. "You need to check in with them every day to find out how they're feeling." Whether it's spending a few minutes talking before they go to bed or chatting with younger kids when they're in the bath, make sure you find time each day to just sit down with your kids. Too young to express emotions? You can always ask him to draw a picture of his feelings for you, adds Lieberman.

6 Plan Family Adventures

Once a week—or as often as you can—set aside some family time and head out to explore something new, says Lieberman. "Rotate who in the family gets to pick what the outing is, so everyone gets a chance to do something special that they like," she adds. Think: Hitting an aquarium or a museum; going to see a show or a movie; taking a hike or picnicking in the woods; or anything else that will give your family some time away from devices to share what's been happening in your lives. These are the moments that will provide your family with the biggest impact and the most lasting memories.

7 Practice Gratitude

Some families say bedtime prayers; others may say grace before dinner. But expressing gratitude can also be worked throughout your child's day, says Supna Shah, founder of WeGo Kids and a mom of triplets based in Tampa, Florida. "In our family, we will practice gratitude several times a day—after a playdate or a trip to the grocery store, in the car, around the house. I'll tell my children two things that

Acknowledging small moments of gratitude—like having time to play together—helps your children become more mindful later in life.

I'm grateful for, like the chance to spend time with the family, and then I'll ask each one what he or she is grateful for. And now my kids will do this unprompted!" says Shah. By acknowledging small moments of gratitude now, she adds, you'll help hardwire your children's brains to recognize and appreciate feelings of thankfulness in their lives.

8 Stop Multitasking

By now, most of us have earned a PhD in the ability to simultaneously juggle tasks (text, cook, help with homework, feed the dog) for the entire family. But you might actually gain more by doing less. Shah recommends the strategy of time blocking. "I block off set amounts of time each day for specific tasks and focus only on those," she says. "When it's my time to be with my kids, I'm with the kids—no distractions allowed. When I'm working, I'm focusing on that." Multitasking may seem like a good way to fit everything in, but ultimately you're adding more stress and not really doing any one thing well. "Kids are born being present, and we grow them out of that all too soon," adds Shah. "It's so important to enjoy every moment and not always be rushing for the next thing."

9 Be Consistent

Consistency is the key to discipline, writes Tanya Altmann, MD, a pediatrician and author of *Baby & Toddler Basics*. And that remains true whether you're dealing with a toddler or a teen. "Set firm limits or consequences for completely unacceptable behaviors," says Altmann. When a younger child throws a temper tantrum, ignore the behavior (walk away, or simply don't pay any attention to her), then after she calms down, refocus your child on something else. And provide praise when your child is behaving nicely, she adds. For older kids, enforce curfews, bedtimes and other age-appropriate limits.

10 Don't Be a Rescue Unit

Admit it—how many times has your kid forgotten her lunch or homework and you've swooped in to save the day by delivering it to her at school or wherever else she may need it? Many of us simply can't stand the thought of our kids being disappointed. But always coming to their rescue can sometimes do more harm than good, says Nicole Beurkens, PhD, a licensed psychologist based in Caledonia, Michigan. "We have to teach kids to be competent and think for themselves," she notes. Whether it's allowing your 3-year-old to dress herself or having your 12-year-old make his bed, give your kids responsibilities and try not to do everything for them.

"Many parents today are not comfortable allowing our kids to be uncomfortable," adds Beurkens. "But in the long run, you're not doing your kids any favors—they need to practice those skills, because in life, you're not always going to be there to help them."

Mistake-Proof Your Parenting

No one's the perfect mom or dad! But here are a few common missteps we all tend to make—and how to avoid them.

Parenting, as every sleep-deprived one of us can attest, is hard work. Wonderful, rewarding, meaningful–and difficult. "Each stage has its challenge, from managing a toddler's tantrums to keeping teens safe from the harms of drugs, alcohol and fast cars," says Rosina McAlpine, PhD, founder of Australia's Win Win Parenting education program in Sydney. Unfortunately, kids don't come with an owner's manual (if only!), and none of us is going to be perfect. But we can learn to avoid some common missteps that parents tend to make by practicing some smart, simple strategies.

When They're Babies

✱ Care for yourself, too.

New moms are usually so busy worrying about everyone else that they don't take the time to care for themselves, says McAlpine. "They try to do it all, but an exhausted and grumpy mom is no fun for anyone. And we know that sleep deprivation can lead to physical- and mental-health issues." So don't be afraid to ask for help, or too proud if someone offers to help out at home.

Taking an occasional short break doesn't mean you're abandoning your duties, agrees David Katzner, president of The National Parenting Center, a nonprofit organization in California that helps provide parenting advice. "Many new parents are gripped by fear or guilt when it comes to leaving their baby with someone, even if it's just [for] a dinner out. You will come back refreshed and reconnected."

✱ Trust your gut.

Don't psych yourself out worrying about everything that might go wrong, advises Katzner. "Parenting an infant, especially your first, can be daunting, overwhelming, exhausting and terrifying. Here's a secret– it doesn't have to be." The infant stage is a "magical time," he adds. "Your baby is learning every day, and you are too." Take a breath, get in touch with your instincts and allow them to guide you. If you're "tense and agonizing over every decision, then you will probably make more mistakes than if you just take a moment and step back."

At the end of the day, agrees McAlpine, the most basic skills are the most important. "The key to raising a happy and healthy baby is for moms and dads to simply respond to their child's needs. Make her feel loved with lots of cuddles and kisses. Feed your baby when he's hungry. Help her go to sleep when she's tired, with a gentle voice and touch.

Support and reassure your baby when he's upset. Help your baby learn by spending quality time together talking, mimicking his facial expressions and sounds, and playing. It's all about building a loving and trusting relationship between parent and child."

When They're Toddlers

✱ Try saying no less often.

Your baby begins to sleep through the night, rewarding you with smiles, laughs and delightful behavior. They've learned to walk and explore the world around them with curiosity and joy. Then the "irrational years" begin, says Katzner. From 18 months up until about 4 years, children discover they are individuals who have the power to refuse us, or even to do the opposite of what we request. In other words, toddlers are supposed to be willful and noncompliant.

But that doesn't mean you have to live with a tiny tyrant. Absolutely go to the mat over the big things, like hitting people or buckling up in the car seat. "Actions speak louder than words. When your child breaks the rules, give her a two-minute time-out. You can't reason with a 2-year-old, so save the speeches," says Katzner. But don't sweat the small stuff. "Keep a sense of humor about this struggle for independence and take some pride in your child's first attempts to stand up for himself."

✱ Keep your cool.

While it may be frustrating to be faced with defiance, anger and punishments inevitably only lead to more tears, tantrums and meltdowns. That doesn't mean that giving in with bribes is the way to stop the meltdown. While that broccoli might be eaten on the promise of ice cream later, parents will soon learn they have trained their children to need a reward to do basic everyday activities like eating healthy food, speaking respectfully and cooperating, says McAlpine.

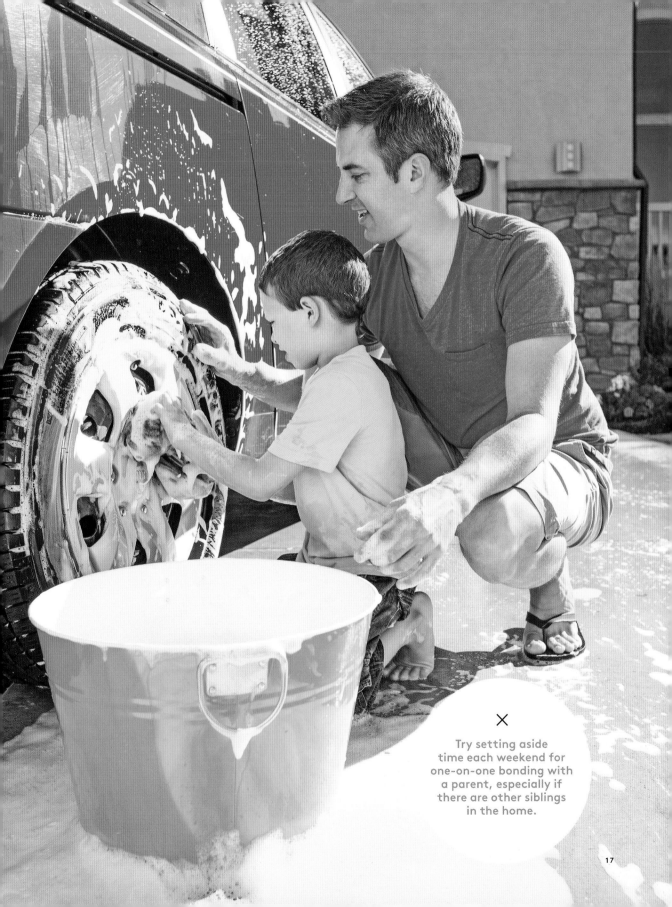

Try setting aside
time each weekend for
one-on-one bonding with
a parent, especially if
there are other siblings
in the home.

Help bickering siblings work out differences by teaching conflict resolution, acknowledging that each of them has a valid perspective.

Instead, try to stay calm, be patient and say yes to your toddler when you can. Whenever possible, give your child choices, such as, "Would you like your dinner on a red plate or the green plate today?" suggests McAlpine. "A little choice can go a long way [toward] a child feeling the autonomy he or she needs."

When They're Preschoolers

✱ Instill lifelong healthy habits.
Childhood obesity has become a major problem. The CDC reports that one in five school-age children in the U.S. is obese, and the rate of obesity has more than tripled since the 1970s. The preschool years are a great time to build healthy nutrition habits that will benefit everyone in the household. Offering kids fresh fruit and vegetables in ready-to-eat, bite-size pieces and limiting processed foods and sugar can help. Being physically active is also good for growing bodies, and it's a fantastic way to use up all that energy kids have! Other healthy habits, including cooking at home, eating meals together when possible and getting enough sleep, will benefit kids in both the short and long term.

✱ Establish chores.
Even at preschool age, it's not too soon to start introducing your child to some simple chores. According to Beth Kobliner, author of *Make Your Kid a Money Genius*, even kids as young as 18 months can do simple chores like hanging up a coat or putting away their shoes. "Research demonstrates that kids who do chores become more successful adults, possibly because of the sense of mastery that they get from a job well done or the feeling of harmony that comes from chipping in as a team player," she writes. As your child gets older, they can take on more household chores around to help out the family. Keep in mind that it's best not to pay your kids for doing chores, advises Kobliner, or suddenly you'll be negotiating how much money it'll take for them to make their beds.

This is also a good opportunity to establish a strong work ethic. "Most people associate the word 'chores' with something unpleasant, something we don't want to do but are forced or bribed to do," says McAlpine. Instead, reframe what chores are and how they work by using positive terms and a positive attitude. "Parents can't expect kids to tidy up after themselves or contribute around the home as a family member and enjoy it, if parents model a negative attitude to home management or are messy. Put some music on; work together to decide who does what tasks and when they are to be done; and start early–young kids love to help," she adds.

When They're in Elementary School

✱ Set firm rules around tech.
With practically every home hosting a slew of technology, from smartphones to consoles and computers, the battle for screen time can feel near-constant. This is one area where parents need to establish firm rules, about the amount of time you're comfortable with your

child having, as well as the content they have access to, advises Katzman. "Your vigilance cannot take a day off, because if you give an inch on this one, your kids will take a mile."

While you're at it, monitor your own media usage. Research shows that too much screen time leads to a decrease in happiness at all ages, and it can also undermine your confidence as a parent. "Nobody puts up their worst moments, nobody's house looks like Pinterest, and every child has different struggles," says Laura Markham, PhD, a clinical psychologist and author of *Peaceful Parent, Happy Kids*. "Minimize your usage of social media, and you will be immeasurably happier."

✳ Be an arbitrator.
Siblings fight–but if that bickering is wearing you down, consider this a good age to teach conflict resolution, says Markham. Don't jump in as judge and jury, or take sides. Simply acknowledge that they both have valid perspectives, then have each hear the other out. Reiterate what you're hearing in a nonaccusatory way and ask them to come up with ideas for a solution. If one kid is being nasty to another, you may need to reiterate the house rules of being kind and respectful

to each other, and they can be coached in communicating in a more direct, less emotional way.

When They're Teens

✳ Keep talking.
Parenting a teen is famously difficult. Teens are risk-taking and thrill-seeking, with brains that are still immature when it comes to thinking ahead about different types of danger and impulsive behavior. That's why it's more important than ever to keep the lines of communication open. "Help teens and tweens to understand the many potential dangers in the world, without scaring the life out of them, and to understand that with freedom comes responsibility," notes McAlpine. That often means curbing the straight-up lecture and encouraging more give-and-take conversation. "Talk to your kids about what they might do to keep themselves safe in various scenarios." You can also help your child focus on finding solutions to problems, rather than ruminating and being stuck, whether it means dealing with a problem at school or coping with a social issue.

✳ Monitor their mental health.
Knowing when your teen's mood swings are normal rather than a cause for concern can be tricky for parents. Warning signs of a serious problem can include: Two or more weeks of feelings of sadness, anxiety and hopelessness; a lack of interest in food or compulsive overeating; changes in sleep habits; social isolation; a sudden drop in grades; cutting school or relentless rebellion; psychosomatic complaints (such as headaches, stomachaches, low-back pain or fatigue); acting out with alcohol, drug use or sexual activity. Suicidal feelings and behaviors are a sign of serious depression, and they require immediate action.

> ✕
> With one in five U.S. school-age children considered obese, it's never too early to start teaching healthy eating habits.

Building Emotional Intelligence

Helping your child identify her feelings—and those
of others around her—not only fosters confidence
but can help set her on a path toward lifelong success.

When one of Supna Shah's 5-year-old triplets gets upset, they don't throw tantrums or hurl a toy across the room. Instead, they'll plop down on the floor, shut their eyes, and start to do some deep breathing.

"I have two boys and a girl, and while they all have very different personalities, each one has learned how to identify emotions such as frustration, anger or fear and have a way to handle those sensations without losing control," says Shah. They've even learned to identify emotions in others. "One of them will come to me and say, 'That boy or girl doesn't look happy–what can I do to make him or her feel better?'"

From a very young age, Shah has worked with her children to refine their emotional intelligence. Also known as EI or emotional quotient (EQ), it's an increasingly popular concept that's found a place in schools, communities and workplaces throughout the country. EI or EQ is typically thought of as a person's ability to recognize, understand and manage both his or her own emotions and to recognize, understand and influence the emotions of others. Although the concept has been around since the 1970s, the EQ movement started to pick up steam in 1996, when science reporter Daniel Goleman published the best-selling book *Emotional Intelligence: Why It Can Matter More Than IQ.*

While some kids may be more instinctively in tune with their EQ, others may need a little more help being taught how to get in touch with their feelings. "It's all about learning how

Breath Control

One of the easiest ways your child can handle emotions like sadness, anger or even excitement is to take a deep breath. "We all need a physical outlet to handle big feelings, and consciously slowing down your breathing can help you do just that," says EQ counselor Supna Shah.

✱ Breathe in as you count to five, filling up your belly as you bring in all that good air.
✱ Slowly breathe out as you count to 10, taking time to empty all the air you can out of your lungs.
✱ Repeat this at least three to five times; more if you need it.

Being able to recognize and understand emotions, even at a young age, can help a child develop empathy and compassion.

✕

Research shows
that teaching EQ
in schools improves
grades and test scores,
and reduces absences
and disciplinary
actions.

People with higher levels of emotional intelligence earn, on average, about $29,000 more a year.

to build an emotional vocabulary so kids can not only talk about their emotions but also understand where they are coming from and what to do with them," explains Ari S. Yares, PhD, a licensed psychologist based in Potomac, Maryland.

More and more schools are also leading the charge in helping students cultivate their EQ throughout the U.S. Today, many districts and even entire states have a curriculum devoted to social and emotional learning (SEL), helping children master the skills of emotional intelligence alongside those of reading comprehension, science and mathematics. In Illinois–which has led the charge to increasing EQ in schools–for example, SEL is integrated into every district's educational programming, from kindergarten through the last year of high school. The goal: to help children develop skills to help calm themselves when angry, make friends, resolve conflicts respectfully and make ethical and safe choices.

The Importance of EQ

It may not sound like much, but developing a high EQ can do more than just help prevent temper tantrums at the grocery store, sibling spats in the back seat of the car, or your teen acting out in high school English class. Teaching kids how to recognize their feelings, see where they are coming from and deal with them are essential life skills, experts say.

And research backs this idea. A meta-analysis of 668 studies of SEL programs for children from preschoolers through high school from the University of Illinois at Chicago found that in schools that incorporated SEL programs, up to 50 percent

of students showed improved achievement scores, and up to 38 percent improved their grade-point average. SEL programs also had an impact on school safety: Reports of misbehavior dropped by an average of 28 percent; suspensions, by 44 percent; and other disciplinary actions, by 27 percent. Meanwhile, attendance rates improved– and 63 percent of students demonstrated significantly more positive behavior.

Plus, the benefits of a high EQ go well past graduation. In Goleman's book, he asserts that IQ (the more conventional measure of intelligence) accounts for only 20 percent of a person's success in life. The other 80 percent may stem largely from the ability to acquire and apply emotional information. An international study from Six Seconds' Institute for Organizational Performance of 665 individuals ranging in ages from 18 to 65 found that more than 54 percent of the variation in success in key areas of life–including achieving results, developing relationships, physical health/ stress management and quality of life–were predicted by EQ.

Shah, who spent more than a decade working in human resources, noticed the importance of a high EQ in the workplace firsthand. "I found that where companies struggle the most is finding people to promote from within, and much of this has to do with developing the characteristics of a good leader, including a high EQ." On average, she says, people with higher levels of emotional intelligence earn $29,000 more a year and are highly sought after by hiring managers. "I found that EQ really is the No. 1 predictor of personal success," she notes.

4 Steps to a Higher EQ

It's almost never too early—or too late—to help your child develop his or her emotional intelligence. Here's how to start.

1

Help your child identify her emotions. Ask your child to put a name to what she's feeling, such as frustration or fear. Labeling emotions helps children take ownership of them and identify not only what they are feeling, but also what others feel. Do this often enough so they have an understanding of what sadness or happiness feels like. For older kids, it can sometimes be hard to get emotional insight. "I don't accept 'I'm OK' as an answer," notes therapist Ari Yares. "We ask kids to create their own words when they don't really know what else to say."

2

Be a good role model. "We adults have to be aware of our own feelings, as well," says Yares. "Often, we don't take the time to listen to our own emotions." After all, the best way to build emotional intelligence is to exhibit it yourself. These don't have to come only from major life events. Tell your children when you are experiencing different emotions, such as being happy because Grandma called or are upset because the carton of eggs fell on the floor. "You can keep it basic, especially for younger kids, but it's important to identify what's going on," adds Yares.

3

Develop an action plan. Some emotions, like anger or fear, require a more immediate response. "It's helpful for kids to understand what to do when they feel certain strong emotions," says Supna Shah. Some children can benefit by doing deep-breathing exercises. (See "Breath Control," p. 22.) Others may find it helpful to draw a picture or to write things down in their own journal. "Any outlet your child can use to express his or her emotions will make a difference in helping craft a response to these types of feelings," adds Shah.

4

Identify how others are feeling. Empathy is a big part of emotional intelligence. For example, if a cashier at the grocery store seems short-tempered or someone cuts your car off in traffic, you can ask your child to identify how that person might be feeling. "It helps them understand that while someone might be rude to them, they have control over how they respond," says Shah. "Once they realize it's not a reflection of them [but] a reflection of that person, it helps build an understanding of how they can react to the emotions of others."

How to Talk to Your Child (So He Really Listens!)

Frustrated by an inability to communicate with your kid? Follow our expert tips to learn how to talk to—not at—your child, and help your message get through loud and clear.

1 Get Up Close

"One of the biggest mistakes parents make is to talk to their kids from another room," notes John Mayer, PhD, a clinical psychologist and parenting consultant based in Chicago. It's natural to tune someone out when they're not even within eyesight. Walk over to your child and make eye contact, which also means asking him or her to put down a device, be it a phone or computer. "It's a lot harder to ignore someone when they are standing in front of you, demanding your attention," says Mayer.

2 Don't Yell

"Once you raise your voice, you've already lost your child's attention," says Mayer. Think about how you would respond in a similar situation, he adds. If your boss came up and started yelling at you, you'd probably start to tune out as well. But if he calmly asked you for your help, you'd likely be a lot more willing to do what he wants. In our house, I notice that the moment I stop yelling and start talking calmly, the more my children will actually pay attention to what I'm saying.

3 Avoid Criticism

"Kids tune you out if you are constantly criticizing them or if you've said the same thing many times before," notes Carole Lieberman, MD, psychiatrist and author of *Lions and Tigers and Terrorists, Oh My! How to Protect Your Child in a Time of Terror.* "To get your child to listen: Take them into a quiet place with few distractions, get them to look at you eye to eye, be direct, and express the importance of what you're saying with the tone of your voice."

4 Don't Be a Broken Record

"Sometimes it can seem like we're teaching our children not to listen, simply by repeating the same request over and over again," says Roseanne Lesack, PhD, a licensed psychologist based in Fort Lauderdale, Florida. If you tell your child to do something, like clearing the table or making his bed, give him some time to comply and then offer to help do it together. "This way, you can make sure they follow through without having to repeat yourself over and over," adds Lesack.

Making direct eye contact when you're talking can help ensure what you're saying gets through to your child.

Make regular one–on–one conversations part of your routine so that your child feels comfortable sharing information with you.

5 Remember That Boys and Girls Are Different

"There is a fundamental difference between most boys and girls when it comes to communication," observes Fran Walfish, PsyD, a child, couple and family psychotherapist in Beverly Hills, California. After about age 7, girls tend to become more verbal; boys often respond better to more visual communications. Emphasize actions (like washing your hands before coming to the dinner table) while praising every increment in your child's autonomy, no matter their age or gender.

6 Act Like a Detective

Nine times out of 10, in my house, if I ask one of my kids how his or her day went, I'll get a one-word answer (usually "OK," "fine" or "good.") And all too often, that's about the extent of the conversation. The key, says Walfish, is to ask more thought-provoking questions, such as "What was your biggest challenge today?" or "What was your favorite thing that you learned about at school?" Once you get the conversation flowing, it's easy to ask follow-up questions and get more information about what's really going on in their lives.

7 Practice Conversation Skills

"Use dinnertime to discuss your day with your children," says Lesack. Younger kids, especially, have a wide development range when it comes to speaking skills. "Try to move away from the 'interview,' or just asking questions of your kids, to a back-and-forth conversation," says Lesack. "Give them some examples of what conversation can look like by sharing stories from your day, like a funny thing that happened to you at work, or have them ask you questions about your day and share that information."

8 Be a Good Listener

"No matter how old they are, kids want to be heard," says Joy Acosto, a parent-child relationship specialist and psychotherapist based in Miami. Take time to hear what they have to say, even if they are pushing boundaries. "Your child may test the waters to see if he or she can be heard or express themselves in unusual ways. The first priority is to help them be able to feel safe in what they are saying –even if it seems outrageous."

9 Make Time to Talk

It can be difficult to find time–especially during busy days–to sit down one-on-one, but parents need to check in regularly with their kids to make sure everything is going OK at school, with friends or in other areas of their lives, says Acosto. "Conversations can help build up a sense of trust–and once you have that trust, your kids are more likely to be open with you and to cooperate."

Teens can be notoriously closed-off from sharing their feelings, but regular check-ins really do help.

The Power of Defiance

Toddlers shout "no!" Teenagers flout curfews.
It's maddening, but your child's disobedience
is a natural—and important—developmental step.

I don't want to!" "I'm not going!" There are times when every parent hears those unwelcome words and inwardly groans, "Why can't you just do what I ask for once?" The answer, many experts have found, is sometimes that your child simply can't. Some level of defiance of authority is a part of childhood, and of maturation, and it comes out in different ways over the years.

The image that usually comes to mind is of a toddler having a meltdown in the grocery store, but acts of defiance and pushback against parents will recur as your child moves through each stage in her development. As a general rule, though, "It's often when kids feel controlled and pushed around that they become defiant," says Laura Markham, PhD, founding editor of ahaparenting.com and author of *Peaceful Parent, Happy Kids*. And of course, children have those feelings often, because they–especially very young ones–do indeed often have little control over their lives. Who wouldn't be frustrated sometimes?

Turn "no" to "yes" by listening and empathizing.

Tapping into that empathy is your first step toward dealing constructively with your child's obstruction. He's arguing because he's frustrated. "Your mantra should be, 'If my child could do better, he would,'" advises parent coach Meghan Leahy. "It's a powerful parenting move to acknowledge that your kid is doing the best he can, and that punitive consequences won't teach him anything." It also helps to understand why your 3-year-old—or 11-year-old, or 15-year old— is pitching a fit. Here's a breakdown of what's going on—and how to deal.

Toddlers

Children's brains are not developed enough to deliberately inhibit certain behaviors or control impulses until around 27 months of age, says Sam Wang, PhD, an associate professor of neuroscience at Princeton University. It is between ages 2 and 3 that she can begin to use her "inside voice" when asked to pipe down, or to keep her hands out of the cookie jar (at least for a while). That means that when she feels strong emotions, like frustration, she can't help but express them. It also means that the idea of "punishment" or "discipline" is beside the point—even if she wanted to, your 2-year-old wouldn't be able to fully control herself.

At about the same time, though, she is developing a sense of herself as separate from her parents, and the first thing she wants to do is show it. Her divergence from you reinforces her growing independence, but she also intermittently fears that separateness, because she knows she is helpless in the world. The result: conflicting signals!

"Defiance happens when the child feels disconnected from the parent," says Markham. "Punishment will just make the disconnection worse. You have to address the defiance, but you solve it with connection, not discipline." Toddlers, she explains, have a fierce need to protect the integrity of their newly discovered "selves." "That's why they're so committed to 'No!' and 'Do it myself!'" So instead of challenging that independence, start with trying to give a hug—sometimes that's all a young child needs to reconnect. Or let him know you're listening, not ignoring. "You say no bath. I hear you." Sometimes just being recognized is enough to quell the resistance, says Markham.

You can also reconsider how flexible you are in the moment. Does he really need a bath tonight? Or can you just wash his hands and face today? When you do want to stick to your limits, let him cry and stay calm while acknowledging his pain: "You're crying because you don't want a bath…I understand…I'm here…. When you're done we'll find your boat to play with in the tub. You always like that."

Distracting and deflecting can be good tools at these ages, as well, in part because of your child's short attention span. If you can get him off whatever is angering him and onto something fun–"Let's go get the boat!"–it may all blow over.

School-Age

By elementary school, kids know most of the rules–and understand when they're breaking them. At this age, defiance often comes when they feel parents are being unfair, says Markham. Your school-age child is also often expressing that she doesn't feel heard or connected. So, after addressing any disrespect that your child has shown ("You know we don't speak to each other that way. You must be very upset"), try to get her to talk about

Let him express
his frustration,
so he feels heard.

No, life isn't fair, but as a parent you can use your power gently.

what's really wrong. "So you don't think that's fair? Maybe I'm missing something. Tell me about it." And try to help her find the language to express her anger or frustration: "Oh, so you feel...you wish...it must feel hard that...." Her anger will likely begin to fade when she feels that you're really listening.

"When I visit classrooms or observe student teachers, over and over again I hear adults saying: 'He's just doing it for attention, ignore him,'" says Tamar Jacobson, PhD, an early childhood development and education consultant. "But children need us to listen to them, to validate their feelings and take them seriously–so seeking attention isn't an inherently negative thing." Instead of thinking, "She's just doing this for attention," Jacobson suggests reframing that into, "She's just doing it for relationship."

There are, of course, times when ignoring minor misbehaviors can be effective. When your child is just whining and complaining, responding to her provocations, even in anger, can serve to reinforce the behavior (sometimes even negative attention feels better to a child than no attention). But attention-seeking through defiant behavior can also sometimes be a sign of a fear of abandonment, Jacobson says, part of that push–pull of independence versus vulnerability. In that case, the best thing you can do is reassure your child that you're there for her.

Tweens and Teens

Enter peer pressure, and a whole new level of defiance–not to mention a whole new vocabulary around it. Your middle schooler or high schooler is pushing back on your limits, not only because he's fighting for his own independence ("Mom, I'm old

enough to...fill-in-the-blank!"), but because he's hearing heroic tales of parental battles from his friends. At times it can seem like teenhood is literally defined by defiance.

One sanity-saver, says Markham, is to remember that "you don't have to attend every power struggle you're invited to." Certainly outright disrespect has to be countered– not with anger, but with calm and honest communication. Job No. 1 (and the hardest part): Take a breath, even though your buttons are being pushed. Then, says Markham, try to translate your teen's defiant words. "She might sound like she never wants to see you again, but underneath her rudeness she's saying, 'I'm all alone out here and pretty miserable.... I wish you'd find a way to come get me, because I don't know how to find my way back." Certainly, that's not what it sounds like when she's shrieking at you, but it may well be what she feels. (Remember that book about tweens titled *Get Out of My Life, but First Could You Drive Me and Cheryl to the Mall?*)

Start with something like, "Ouch! That was pretty rude...you must be very upset to speak to me that way. What's going on?" (Of course, this presumes that you have been modeling respectful speech to your child, adds Markham. If you haven't been, this is the moment to admit it, apologize and say that everyone in the family needs to turn over a new leaf.) Then stay compassionate while he expresses why he is upset: "Wow... I see...I'm so sorry...I didn't realize." He may largely need to tell you about all his built-up feelings that have been making him feel so disconnected from you.

The good part about defiance at these ages, though, is that–even though your child's rational decision-making frontal cortex isn't fully developed yet–he has a lot more reasoning power than he did at 3 or at 10. Try to find a "win-win" or compromise, and map out a solution together. The goals should be empathy, finding common ground and problem-solving so you both get your needs met, says Markham. Yes, it's more easily said than done, especially when the scene involves slamming doors and raised voices and a cauldron of puberty hormones.

Lastly, whatever the age of your child, think of defiance as an opportunity, not an emergency. "Most of us get so triggered by our child's defiance that we automatically come down like a sledgehammer," says Markham. "And we're thinking: 'I wouldn't have been allowed to act that way when I was young!' But rather than a red flag in front of a bull, your child's defiance is more like a red light on the dashboard of your car–a signal that something is wrong that needs to be fixed. And what's wrong isn't your child, but the relationship. That gets fixed by reconnecting, not by attacking." So go ahead, start a dialogue!

When It's More Serious

What you should know about oppositional defiant disorder

At any given moment, your child's pushback might seem extreme— understandably. Most kids can come back to baseline fairly quickly, but in some children a pattern develops that becomes increasingly problematic either at school, at home or both. It's called oppositional defiant disorder, or ODD, and it is distinguished by a cluster of symptoms. All kids can have these from time to time, but ODD is defined as having had extreme behavior issues for at least six months, including:

* Being unusually angry and irritable
* Frequently losing their temper
* Being easily annoyed
* Arguing with authority figures
* Refusing to follow rules
* Deliberately annoying people
* Blaming others for mistakes
* Being vindictive

A particular hallmark of ODD is the toll it often takes on family relationships, as daily confrontations build up over time, damaging the parent-child bond as both become frustrated and easy to trigger. If you feel your child's behavior might be nearing the boundaries of ODD, consult a mental-health professional who can diagnose it (and any other mental-health issues that might accompany it), and help both parent and child learn effective ways of handling anger and communication.

ODD is tough on kids—and parents.

Rearing Resilient Kids

The ability to bounce back from tough times is
a key life skill—one every child can learn.

In a perfect world, no child would ever feel scared, stressed or hurt. And every child would breeze through the stages of development, and any stray obstacles, without suffering a moment of pain or self-doubt. But in fact, say many experts, that wouldn't be a perfect world at all. Humans–even little ones–actually benefit from a certain amount of stress and difficulty. After all, if you never hit a snag, you never learn how to deal with snags. Being able to take setbacks in stride and still thrive is the definition of resilience. So the question is: Can you help your child develop that quality?

Absolutely, says Amanda Mintzer, PsyD, a psychologist at the Child Mind Institute. "Part of resilience is temperament and

Face fears by uniting the two sides of the brain.

genetics, but it's definitely also something that can be fostered." On the inheritance side, researchers have identified certain genetic variations–affecting the action of the "stress" hormone cortisol, along with the "happiness" neurotransmitter serotonin–that appear to predispose some people to be more resilient when challenged. But studies in rats have shown that such predispositions can be altered by early life experience.

"These are called epigenetic modifications, in which the environment permanently influences the way genes are expressed," explains Sam Wang, PhD, an associate professor of neuroscience at Princeton University. "In rats, maternal behaviors like licking and grooming of pups trigger the release of serotonin in the babies' hippocampus, and that changes the way their brains deal with cortisol. They become more able to shut down stress responses throughout their lives–it's a permanent modification in their DNA."

The effects of early-life stress are similar in humans, rodents and monkeys, Wang adds, so the takeaway is that you can help wire your child's brain for resilience. But that involves different approaches at different ages. Here's what you can do to help.

Induce Trust

Your first gift to your baby is to assure her that you have her back–literally. Infants are helpless, and one of their first tasks is to identify who they can trust to tend to their needs and answer their cries. This is why it's impossible to "spoil" a baby; when she cries and you're there to comfort her, you are triggering the serotonin response that will set up her brain to better deal with

stress and the cortisol surge that comes with it. "Toddlers and older children who are in secure attachment relationships show less elevation of cortisol in response to stress than children in insecure relationships who don't see their parents as a reliable source of comfort," says Wang.

Let Some Stress Happen

As your toddler begins interacting with the world at large, he needs to find ways of comforting himself. A little stress, it turns out, helps that occur. "Children develop their coping skills most effectively if they are exposed to a moderate amount of stress–high enough that they notice it, but low enough that they can handle it," says Wang. Again, animal studies bear out the mechanism, he adds. "Young monkeys separated from their mothers for one hour a week grow up to manage stress more easily than monkeys who were never separated from their mothers." As adults, moderately stressed monkeys had lower levels of stress hormones and anxiety, and did better on a test of prefrontal cortex function. But when separated for several hours a day, animals grow up more anxious and stressed, and slower to learn.

Your child grows more through challenges than through protection.

Fear, excitement
and confidence are
all connected.

Face fears by uniting the two sides of the brain.

"It's called hormesis," explains Louann Brizendine, MD, a neuropsychiatrist. "When your cells are intermittently stressed, they become more resilient." It's like exercise, where you stress a muscle and cause a little damage in the short term, but in the long term, the muscle is stronger. In the emotional realm, says Brizendine, "Once you weather something in your life, you know you've made it through–and that gives you confidence for the next big stressor. The key is having 'just enough' stress so you can recover well."

Model Resilience for Your Child

"Never forget that children are sponges, and from a very early age," says Mintzer. "They see, hear and pick up on everything around them. Modeling resilience for your child involves the language you use, not just to them but around them." Let them see you dealing with challenges in a calm and confident manner, and label it: "Yes, waiting in line at the post office is frustrating–I'm frustrated! But we need to mail our letter."

Be open about your mistakes as well, so your child sees they're a normal part of life and not a disaster. Acknowledge that something didn't work out the way you wanted, and that you're disappointed but not crushed: It's just part of life.

Celebrate Effort and Perseverance

"All of the literature about grit and resilience emphasizes not only how we talk to our kids, but what we praise them for," says Mintzer. "It's about praising appropriately and effectively–praising the effort, not just the end result." Accomplishments are fine to celebrate, of course, but many skills require hard work that takes time. By paying attention to the process, you're encouraging them to see the whole endeavor as a positive.

It's also about embracing the less-than-perfect–in your life, in your child's, or in something on TV. In these social media days, when many strive for a "perfect" image, it's key to pull the veil off that fantasy. Chasing perfection can lead your child to lose patience with setbacks, or hesitate to try things that may not immediately succeed.

Talk About Trauma

When a child has had an upsetting experience, many parents assume it's best to reassure him that it's OK and then deflect or distract. But according to Daniel J. Siegel, MD, and Tina Payne Bryson, PhD, co-authors of T*he Whole-Brain Child*, talking through the experience with your child–often many times–is very helpful. The two psychologists call it "name it to tame it," and it helps your child unite her left brain (rational and verbal) with her right brain (emotional and nonverbal). She'll use this skill to deal with upsets for the rest of her life, from falling off a bicycle to the trauma of a major loss. "The right side of our brain processes emotional memories, but our left side makes sense of these feelings," Siegel and Bryson write. "Healing emerges when the sides work together to tell our life stories."

Putting words to it begins to "tame" the emotions, and research shows that labeling what we feel calms the brain's emotional circuitry. Encourage your child to do this, walking through it with her and offering support, and she will learn to return to equilibrium–the very definition of a resilient child.

Time to Ground the Parental Helicopter?

Many parents today are much more involved in their children's lives than in previous generations—and research shows that's not always a good thing.

The current generation of parents deserves credit for being considerably more "present" for their children than in previous times, according to Gail Saltz, MD, of the Child Mind Institute. "That's important in order to nurture a child," she says. "But this generation has also taken active parenting to new competitive heights." Enter the Helicopter Parent, the one hovering over every moment of her child's life, making sure nothing untoward occurs (and the newest addition, the Snowplow Parent—for example, the wealthy couples caught up in the college-admissions bribery scandal—who seek to actively clear all obstacles for their children).

Research is emerging that such overly involved parenting can actually hold your child back, especially as he grows into adulthood. One study, published in the journal *Developmental Psychology*, found that children whose parents were overcontrolling (described as constantly guiding their child by telling him or her what to play with, how to play with a toy, how to clean up after playtime and being too strict or demanding) had more trouble regulating their emotions and behavior as they grew older—key skills for success both at school and socially. "Children with helicopter parents may be less able to deal with the challenging demands of growing up, especially with navigating the complex school environment," says lead author Nicole B. Perry, PhD, from the University of Minnesota.

Another study found that parents of anxious children tried to help their child more than parents whose child wasn't anxious, even when the child didn't ask for support. In other words, the parents saw the challenges faced by their kids as more threatening than the children did. Over time, this reduced the children's natural ability to succeed using their own initiative. That kind of over-involvement can even cause anxiety in some children. Other research shows that college students who said their parents were actively involved in their schoolwork, or created very structured environments during their youth, were more likely to have depression and anxiety as adults, and were also less likely to persevere with difficult tasks.

Parents need to keep their kids safe, but also know when to give them space.

CHAPTER 2

Keeping Kids Healthy

We can't protect our little ones from every scratch and sniffle, but with a little planning we can boost mind, body and spirit.

Food for Thought

Feeding your kids isn't just about getting dinner on the table—it's teaching them to eat well and establish healthy nutrition habits at every age.

From the moment a child is born, we often start obsessing about what she'll eat. (Breast or bottle? Scheduled or on-demand feedings?) And as she grows and her diet expands, it's up to you to not only provide the type and amount of food, but also to establish healthy nutrition habits that will last a lifetime. "Children typically learn their eating habits from their parents. And the goal is to raise children with a positive relationship with food," notes Michelle

Dudash, RDN, creator of 4Real Food Reboot, a healthy-meal-planning program. To give your kid some nutrition savvy, follow these eating guidelines for every age.

Infants

6–12 MONTHS

* **Establish healthy habits.** Though you'll be feeding your baby breast milk or formula for about the first six months, after that it's time to start introducing solids. And the habits babies learn about eating now will stick with them for life. "When you're weaning and introducing solids, that will set up their relationship to eating," says Marina Chaparro, RDN, a spokeswoman for the Academy of Nutrition and Dietetics and founder of Nutrichicos, a website dedicated to nutrition and wellness for children. "Kids are responsible for deciding how much they eat and if they want to eat it. As parents, you're the ones deciding what food you're going to present. Once you have that established, you create a healthier relationship for feeding."

And while it may be tempting to try to get your baby to finish every bite, it's important not to force-feed children from a young age, adds Chaparro. "Babies are very intuitive and know how much they need to eat, even at this early stage."

* Mix things up. A baby's first solids usually start with cereal. Then work your way up to fruits, vegetables, eggs, dairy, meat and seafood, plus thin layers of nut and seed butters. The more variety, the better. "There's a window of opportunity now, because your baby is still learning about foods," says Chaparro. "At this age, kids are very open, so introduce lots of fruits and veggies and flavors."

* Be bold. Avoid giving bland combos out of fear your baby won't like anything else— and don't avoid certain foods just because you happen to dislike them. "Even different textures are important at this age," says Chaparro. She recommends an iron-rich diet (think: beans, chicken, eggs, meat, lentils and fortified cereal), since it plays a major role in neurological and cognitive development. Foods to steer clear of at this age include honey, due to the potential risk of botulism; choking hazards, such as popcorn, nuts, hard candy and dried fruits; and cow's milk, which should be introduced only after 12 months of age.

Toddlers & Preschoolers

`1-4 YEARS`

* Have patience. There's a reason it's called the Terrible Twos. "This is the time when kids are flourishing in independence," says Chaparro. "They have learned the word *no* and have more of a personality and a say." Your child also isn't growing at the same rate as when he was an infant, so expect his appetite to be on and off. "Kids might eat a lot one day and very little the next," says Chaparro. Repetition is also a big trend. Your child might want to eat mac and cheese every day for a week and then suddenly hate it. "The most important tip is don't give up. They might not eat what you're offering today, but next month, they might love it."

* Offer choices. Support their newfound independence but foster healthy eating by giving healthy options–like deciding whether they want bananas or blueberries. Toddlers' plates should be loaded with whole grains, fruits, vegetables, eggs, dairy (whole milk for 1-year-olds, low-fat for ages 2 and up), meat and seafood. Make sure they're getting plenty of calcium and healthy fats for development–for example, olive oil; peanut butter; 2 percent milk; and foods rich in omega-3 fatty acids, such as salmon, which will help with brain development. Get creative: Turn scrambled eggs, fruit and toast into a funny face, or use a cookie cutter to make cute shapes with vegetables–whatever it takes to make the food more enticing.

* Be consistent. Now is the time to establish regular meal times–and not the constant noshing that can undermine nutrition. "Put your child on a healthy schedule, which should be three meals and two or three snacks per day," advises Dudash. And don't worry about them cleaning their plates. "Allow your child to eat until he or she has had enough."

✕

Research shows
that early introduction
of peanut products can
decrease the chance that
a child will develop
a future peanut
allergy.

Once teens hit puberty, their protein needs become even more important for producing critical enzymes and hormones.

✳ **Let 'em grow.** Not much changes by way of diet once toddlers reach preschool age, except the choking hazard restrictions no longer apply. "It's just the portion sizes and number of servings that increase," Dudash says. Continue to offer variety, with plenty of fresh fruits and vegetables as well as healthy fats and whole grains.

School Age

`5–9 YEARS`

✳ **Be a good role model.** Now that your child is a little older, it's more important than ever to set a good example. Instead of lecturing kids about what not to eat, lead by example, making sure your own diet is filled with healthy choices and appropriate portions. And avoiding labeling, warns Dudash. "I don't recommend getting into 'healthy' or 'unhealthy,' since this can have negative consequences, like unfavorable views toward healthy foods or a fear of unhealthy foods," she says.

✳ **Get them involved.** Now's also a good time for your child to be more hands-on. Let him help prepare dinner or his school lunches. Go to the grocery store together. "Put food choices into their daily lives," says Dudash. The more your child is exposed to how food gets to his plate, the better the eating habits he'll develop.

✳ **Serve healthy snacks.** Snacks serve an important purpose at this age, especially if you have a finicky eater in the house. But they shouldn't be an excuse just to nosh. "Snacks are there to supplement nutrition requirements and complement meals," says

Chaparro. "It's hard for children to meet 100 percent of their nutritional needs just at mealtime, so choosing healthy, nutrient-dense snacks helps fill in the gaps." Focus on whole foods, like fruits and veggies; whole grains; and proteins, such as cheese, Greek yogurt or hummus.

Tweens

`10–12 YEARS`

✳ **Stay positive.** It's never a good idea to talk about weight, a restrictive diet, or food in a negative way, but that's especially true once kids hit the middle school age. "We know that kids' perception of their bodies starts at about age 5," Chaparro says. "If we are constantly talking with a 5-year-old about her weight, then in the preteen or teen years we often find issues." Those can include body image distortion, dieting, compulsive exercising, body shaming and other forms of eating disorders.

✳ **Dine in.** You'll always be looking over their shoulder, so put an emphasis on the family dinner every night, where you control the menu. Research shows that having just two to three family dinners a week has been shown to reduce obesity. Chaparro recommends serving calcium-rich dishes often, especially if you have girls, since two-thirds of teen girls don't get enough of it. Find it in dairy like milk and cheese, fish like sardine and salmon, and dark, leafy greens like kale and bok choy.

Teens

`13–19 YEARS`

✳ **Find protein power.** Protein is also especially important during the tween and teen stages because it builds, maintains and supports tissue growth. If you have a young athlete, protein is vital for building muscle; but any growing teen–especially once they hit puberty–needs adequate protein, since it also plays a role in the production of enzymes and hormones. Aim for about 0.85 grams of protein per kilogram of body weight (for a 135-pound kid, that's about 52 grams daily).

* Reinforce good habits. Offer the healthiest options possible for meals your kids eat at home, which are typically breakfasts and dinners. "Sometimes we think that because the food is there they are going to eat it, but teens are not really adults–they don't have that same mental capacity," Chaparro says. Since they're into grab-and-go, cut up fruit like apples or berries beforehand, buy healthy granola or energy bars, or make egg frittatas to freeze for later. At some point, your teen will have to make his own choices. "Providing is all you can do. Whether they choose to eat healthy is up to them," says Chaparro.

New Rules

Raise healthy eaters by following these nutrition guidelines.

`DO` **Create a schedule.** Food shouldn't be a 24/7 free-for-all. "There should be set times for meals and snacks—and no eating in front of the screen," says Michelle Dudash, RDN.

`DON'T` **Treat food as a reward.** Promising your little one a cookie if he eats his broccoli is never a good idea. "You're basically saying broccoli is the worst thing ever and that if you eat it, you can get this," says Marina Chaparro, RDN. "And never associate food with some type of behavior."

`DO` **Let kids decide how much to eat.** "Children are actually quite good at self-regulation, as long as they aren't mindlessly munching away," Dudash says. "Teach them that when they are hungry, they will get as much as they want to be satisfied."

`DON'T` **Put your kid on a diet.** "It's better to put an emphasis on the deliciousness of healthy foods," says Dudash. Rather than limiting calories, the American Academy of Pediatrics recommends healthy levels of physical activity.

`DO` **Make food fun.** Start your own cooking contests. "Try setting up a night where parents and kids are the judges of what that meal tasted like," says Chaparro. "Make it into a game. It's a fun way of introducing new foods and veggies instead of just telling them to try it because it's good for you."

`DON'T` **Make food a big deal.** "Congratulating children for eating well and scolding kids for when they're not eating what's expected draws too much attention to the food," Dudash says.

Why Good Sleep Habits Are Key

Regardless of how old—or young—your kids are, they (and you!) could benefit from learning to catch some high-quality Z's.

I still remember the day my daughter decided that she didn't want to sleep at night anymore. She was almost 6 months old; we were on a trip to Bend, Oregon; and my husband and I had been fooled into believing that she was naturally a pretty good sleeper. Before then, she might wake up once–maybe twice–a night, but she always went back down fairly easily, and we seemed to manage to catch just enough shut-eye to operate like "normal" people the next day.

Then all of a sudden, something changed. She changed. She started crying at around midnight, and we shushed her back down.

At 2 a.m., repeat. Then at 4 a.m. Then...well, you get the picture. It was like we accidentally set an alarm clock to go off every two hours. I had to wake up at 6 a.m. to do a 5k race, and I honestly didn't think I could consume enough coffee to get me to the finish line in an upright position. Somehow, I managed. And on the drive home, I thought, "Well, that was terrible. But maybe it was just because we were traveling." Unfortunately, I was wrong. Sleep became a sometimes nightly battle for the next four-plus months. I now know that despite the fact that she was sleeping fairly well in the beginning, we still should have armed our daughter with some tools that could have (maybe, probably) helped make things easier later on.

"Sleep health is like building blocks– parents can start putting them in place one piece at a time, beginning when their children are newborns," says Jodi Mindell, PhD, a professor at Saint Joseph's University in Philadelphia and associate director of the Sleep Center at Children's Hospital of Philadelphia. "It's so important, since sleep affects all aspects of our well-being. If your kid isn't getting enough sleep, it can affect their mood, behavior, cognition and overall health." Whether you're just getting started or simply feel like you've gotten off course, don't worry. It's never too late to start building good sleep habits.

Infants & Toddlers

✳ Create a routine. It doesn't really matter what your routine is, so long as you're being consistent from night to night. "This is key for establishing good sleep habits from as early as when your baby is a few months old," says Mindell. For a newborn, the routine may simply include a bath, a diaper change, milk and a lullaby before bed. For a toddler, it could be bath, pajamas, brushing teeth and a book.

Getting a good night's sleep affects mood, behavior, cognition and overall health.

Just like adults, kids' rooms should be set up for good sleep hygiene by being kept cool, dark, quiet and free of electronics.

✳ Set the clock. "Establish regular sleep/wake patterns as early as possible (once there is some regular pattern that emerges), so that you can teach your child the importance of routines and bedtime–and set appropriate expectations for sufficient sleep and rest," says Sally Ibrahim, MD, a sleep medicine specialist at the Cleveland Clinic in Cleveland. And if they start to push back (as they often do), resist the urge to let them stay up later.

✳ Give them a bath (but not too early). Taking a warm bath will raise your child's core body temperature; when she gets out, her body temp naturally drops, which enhances the drowsiness response, explains Jerald Simmons, MD, a neurologist and sleep-medicine specialist in Houston. However, this benefit lasts only 45 minutes to an hour, so aim to put them to bed during that window, he adds.

✳ Encourage self-soothing. "If an infant gets used to being held or fed to fall asleep, then they'll expect it to happen every time they wake up at night and will cry until that condition is reintroduced," says Ibrahim. Babies make associations quickly, so create a sleep routine that doesn't rely on a family member, and allows your child to self-soothe instead. Try to put your child to bed while drowsy but awake. If this leads to a "cry it out" situation, remind yourself that while it's incredibly hard, it won't last forever.

✳ Don't disregard naps. Trouble with daytime naps can mean trouble at night as well, so it's important to be consistent and follow an abbreviated bedtime routine for these as well. According to the National Sleep Foundation, when it's time for your toddler to drop one (or all!) naps, you should ease into the change gradually and consider turning what would be nap time into a new quiet time, when your kid can read books, color or listen to calming music.

Preadolescents

✳ Get outside. "Melatonin helps your brain go to sleep, and your levels of it change when your body is exposed to different types of light," explains Simmons. "Levels are lower when it's bright and higher when it's dark." But it's the fluctuation in levels between day and night that provide great sleep-inducing benefits, he adds–so if you're inside all day, you'll miss out, making it more difficult to fall asleep.

✳ Shut down electronics. "Research shows that implementing a consistent bedtime is associated with adequate sleep, even in adolescents," says Ibrahim. So it's important to impose limitations on things that may get in the way of their shut-eye, such as phones or computers, and to dim the lights in their room at night. One recent study found that kids who used digital devices before bed were more likely to get less sleep and have a higher BMI than their tech-free peers.

✳ Don't ignore daytime behavior. Sleep issues can pop up at any time, and they're not always obvious to spot. Ask yourself, "How's my child's daytime performance?" If they seem tired all the time and you're noticing he or she is struggling at school or elsewhere, then you might want to talk to a sleep specialist, notes Simmons. Also, snoring is abnormal at any age. "If your child isn't sleeping through the night or is breathing heavily while he sleeps, talk to your pediatrician about the possibility of sleep apnea," says Ibrahim.

Teens

✳ Wake them up. "Some parents allow their kids to sleep in as long as possible on the weekends, but it's important to maintain a regular schedule," says Ibrahim. "Your best bet is to keep sleep/wake times within an hour or two of normal. Otherwise, kids can end up with social 'jet lag' on Sunday night, which makes it hard to go to sleep and creates a snowball effect of late nights and tired days for the rest of the week."

✳ Keep messaging to a minimum. Try to get your teens to shut down for the night before they enter their bedrooms. "If they're texting or staying digitally engaged with their friends, then they'll never drift off. Turn off their phones, tablets, etc.," says Simmons. Better yet, keep the electronic devices out of the bedroom altogether and charge them in another room.

✳ Make sleep a rou-teen. Less sleep time for teens has been associated with car accidents, mood disturbances and other high-risk behaviors, such as smoking, notes Ibrahim. Yet with all the social–and scholastic–pressures that come with being in high school, lots of teenagers are at least a little sleep-deprived. "The biological sleep patterns for adolescents and teens shift toward later sleep/wake times, so it's natural for them to not be able to fall asleep earlier," explains Simmons. "However, we all function better with a routine, when our body knows what to expect."

–Lindsey Emery

How Many Z's Does Your Kid Need?

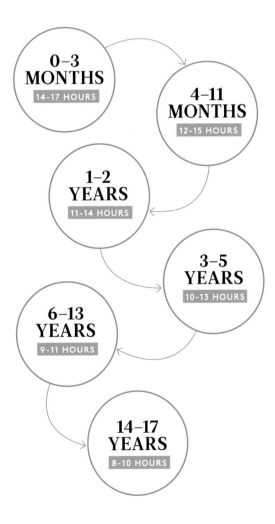

* Recommended daily sleep guidelines from the National Sleep Foundation

Only about one in five 6- to 19-year-olds gets the recommended hour or more of moderate to vigorous physical activity at least five days a week.

Movement Matters

Physical activity is vital to your child's development
at every age and stage.

Your child is built to move. From the moment they start to gain control over their bodies, babies are hardwired to lift themselves up; roll back and forth; sit up; crawl; stand; and eventually walk, run and climb. By the time they are 2, most kids are racing about, kicking balls and tearing it up on tricycles with no signs of slowing down.

Except all too often, our kids do just that. Whether it's the lure of the screen or limited time outside of school, homework and other extracurriculars, kids are less active today than ever: Just 21.6 percent of 6- to 19-year-olds in the U.S. get 60 or more minutes of moderate-to-vigorous physical activity at least five days a week, according to the Centers for Disease Control and Prevention (CDC).

"Physical activity is beneficial for all ages, but for kids it's especially important," notes Magdalena Oledzka, DPT, director of pediatric rehabilitation at the Hospital for Special Surgery in New York City. "It stimulates growth; strengthens muscles; builds strong bones; boosts cardiovascular health; prevents obesity; and improves cognitive functions like memory, processing speed and attention." Movement is so important that the government's Guidelines for Physical Activity report now recommends that children as young as age 3 accumulate at least 60 minutes of activity each day.

But don't think you have to sign your kid up for her own gym membership by the time she's out of diapers. "Young kids thrive on unstructured play, so we want to encourage our kids to do any activity they can in a safe environment," says Len Saunders, educator and author of *Generation Exercise*. And don't be scared off by the one-hour guideline. "It doesn't have to mean doing 60 minutes of physical activity all at once." Think: walking 10 minutes to and from school, 20 minutes running in the playground and 20 minutes playing in the backyard. "It all adds up." Try these other strategies for helping kids increase their activity levels.

Infants

You may not think movement is terribly important when your baby can't even crawl, but even infants can start to build the strength and skills they need to thrive. That starts with giving your baby plenty of supervised tummy time. "Take babies out of the bouncy seat, car stroller, swing and other containers and allow them to get on a mat on both their back and belly so they can start to practice rolling around," says Oledzka. This not only helps strengthen important muscles, it also helps prevent plagiocephaly, or flat head syndrome, and improves gross motor skills and vision development. Aim for about an hour of tummy time a day. (Break this into smaller 10- to 15-minute chunks; few infants can last an hour at a time.)

Toddlers

"For toddlers, fitness is really playtime," says Oledzka. Play is how kids learn about themselves and the world around them, and it's how many social and cognitive skills are developed. "Parents often think even young kids' days need be scheduled from the moment they wake up until bedtime, but they also need time to just play," says Catherine Tamis-LeMonda, PhD, professor of applied psychology at New York University. Her research shows that more than half of a toddler's wake time is spent playing with toys and other objects. "Kids play with everything, from boxes and bottles to traditional toys. It's a way for them to see how things fit together and practice fine motor skills, spacial concepts and other important developmental skills."

So give your toddler lots of time to run around. "Often, once a child can start to walk, they won't sit still," adds Tamis-LeMonda. And all that movement helps them grow. "Running from room to room may not look like it has much purpose, but it all feeds into cognitive and motor development."

Preschoolers

As kids get a little older, physical activity becomes even more important to both development and socialization. "Young kids still have this innate drive to move," says Oledzka. But many preschoolers spend hours a day planted in front of the TV or staring at a device instead of running around. In fact, our preschoolers today are only about one-fourth as active in their day-to-day lives as their grandparents were, according to the American Academy of Pediatrics. Building in playtime with games and sports helps improve motor skills and coordination. Help things along by offering age-appropriate equipment like balls and plastic bats, scooters, bikes or trikes. Get the whole family in on the act–take a short hike on the weekend, play tag, head for the park–whatever you can do to move together.

Elementary School

Once kids hit kindergarten, they're often spending hours at a time sitting still. "This is when it's more important than ever to keep promoting movement," says Oledzka. Not every kid is a natural athlete, so that doesn't necessarily mean signing up for Little League or skating lessons. Find activities that best interest your child, considering her

✕

Preschoolers today are only about 25 percent as active as their grandparents were, thanks largely to the distraction of electronic devices.

Simple play helps build gross motor skills.

personality, skills, size and interests. "It all revolves around your child's passions," notes Alex Haschen, a personal trainer in Easton, Pennsylvania, and owner of Boost Basics. If your child loves animals, take a hike and see what kind of critters you can spot; if she likes to dance, put on music and have an impromptu party.

"The important thing is to make fun the focus—it's not always about being the best or winning," adds Saunders. "Find an activity that your child enjoys and teach him to always give his best effort and be proud of his accomplishments."

Middle and High School

"Around ages 10 to 12, kids often start slowing down and don't want to run around as much," says Oledzka. Often, movement is limited to organized sports or activities like soccer, ballet or softball. But a twice-weekly practice or class isn't enough activity to help keep them strong and healthy. And some kids don't want to do any organized activity.

So motivate where you can. "If your kid is really into sports, create movement around that with the end goal of improving performance. And if you have a kid who's more interested in schoolwork than soccer, emphasize that physical activity will also help them do better in school," says Haschen.

This might also be a time when your child becomes interested in doing some strength training. Keep things safe by focusing on body-weight exercises at first (like push-ups, pull-ups, sit-ups and squats); for teens, supervised weight training with relatively light weights may also be appropriate. "Just make sure that you are teaching your child proper form, or have them work with a trainer who can show them what to do," adds Saunders. "It's important to learn how to use the right technique so they'll avoid injury and get the results they want."

Team sports aren't for every kid, but all children need regular activity.

12 Ways to Keep Your Family Fit

Get your kids up and moving while getting in on the action for yourself.

1 Create a fitness scavenger hunt. Plant items around the house with notes attached, suggests educator Len Saunders. Each time they find an object, include a fitness challenge, like five push-ups or 10 jumping jacks.

2 Play balloon ball. Try and go for a record on keeping a balloon in the air, says trainer Alex Haschen. For an extra challenge, use only one hand, or just the feet!

3 Try an active game of charades. Make the categories sports, animals, professions and exercises for extra movement, says Haschen.

4 Have a dance-off. Download a playlist and show your kids your best footwork—then watch them do theirs.

5 Curb tech time. Give your kids a goal to earn their screen time by instituting a rewards system. For every 30 minutes of activity (like going on a family walk or a bike ride) give them 15 minutes of screen time, advises Saunders.

6 Find some indoor entertainment. Whether it's bad weather or just boredom, try hitting the trampoline or skate park, or head for the rec center. "Sometimes it just helps to get out of the house and do something new," says Haschen.

7 Use commercial time wisely. Get the whole family off the couch during commercial breaks and do exercises like jumping jacks or push-ups—or try to hold a plank pose (the "up" part of a push-up).

8 Compete in a family push-up challenge. See if your family can set a goal of each doing 50 push-ups in a day. It doesn't have to be all at once, says Haschen. For example: Do 10 push-ups when you get out of bed, another 5 before breakfast, another 5 after breakfast, 10 after school, 5 before dinner, 5 after dinner and 10 more about 20 minutes before bedtime. (Modify as necessary.)

9 Hoop it up. Get those Hula-Hoops out and practice your twirling. You can do this without needing a lot of space. Find out who can keep it going the longest!

10 Have a beanbag challenge. Walk around the house with a small beanbag or pillow balanced on your head, or try going up and

down the stairs without using your hands to hold it in place. Or you can have a beanbag catch— or try setting up some plastic water bottles and making your own "beanbag bowling" alley.

11 **Try some yoga.** There's no shortage of family-friendly yoga videos you can download to get everyone in on the asana, and kids love doing some animal poses like lion's face or downward dog. Or just put on some relaxing music and practice deep breathing and stretches—they're perfect before bedtime.

12 **Build your own indoor obstacle course.** Rainy day making your kids nuts? Challenge them to get through a DIY course. Try running up stairs, jumping over pillows, crawling under a broom that's propped up on low tables. "Use anything in your house to get your kids jumping, running, crawling or climbing!" says Haschen.

Sick–Kid Rescue Plan

Upset tummy? Runny nose? Here's what to do
when your child is feeling under the
weather—and when it's time to bring in the pros.

Bloody Nose

KEY SYMPTOMS

Bleeding from nose

TREATMENT

* Have your child tilt his head slightly
  forward; gently blow nose
* Pinch lower half of child's nose,
  hold firmly for 10 minutes

CALL A DOCTOR IF...

* Your child is losing too much blood
* Bleeding is coming only from the mouth,
  or your child is coughing or vomiting
  blood or brown material
* Your child is pale and sweaty
  or unresponsive

Bug/Insect Bites or Stings

KEY SYMPTOMS

Stinging sensation followed by small,
red, itchy bumps or marks

TREATMENT

* For bites by mosquitoes, flies, fleas
  and bedbugs: Apply cool compress and

calamine lotion or use a low-potency topical steroid. For children over age 6, an oral antihistamine (like Benadryl) can help control the itch

* For wasp or bee stings: Soak a cloth in cold water, press it over the area of the sting to reduce pain and swelling. Remove bee stinger quickly (gently scrape it off horizontally with a credit card or use a clean fingernail). Pediatric acetaminophen or ibuprofen (for a child over 6 months) can reduce pain

CALL A DOCTOR IF...

* Symptoms persist or become difficult to control
* If the bite looks like it has become infected (becomes redder, larger, more swollen)
* Call 911 if: Your child has sudden difficulty breathing; is weak; collapses or becomes unconscious; develops hives or itching all over body; vomits; has extreme swelling near eyes, lips or penis that makes it difficult for child to see, eat or urinate

Cold/Upper Respiratory Infection

KEY SYMPTOMS

Runny nose, sneezing, mild fever (101–102°F), reduced appetite, sore throat, cough, slightly swollen glands in neck

TREATMENT

* Use saline nose drops or spray for nasal congestion. For an infant, suction congestion with rubber suction bulb
* Use a cool-mist humidifier or vaporizer in room at night
* Give your child plenty of fluids
* Make sure your child gets lots of rest
* If your child is older than 6 months and has a fever, administer acetaminophen or ibuprofen (pediatric version)

CALL A DOCTOR IF...

* Your baby is less than 3 months old: With a young infant, symptoms can be

Scientists believe that a fever is the body's way of fighting germs that cause infections by making it a less hospitable place for them to stay.

Most kids with a temperature of less than 102˚F don't need medicine, unless they are uncomfortable.

misleading, and colds can quickly develop into more serious ailments, such as bronchitis, croup or pneumonia

* Lips or nails turn blue
* Nasal mucus lasts for more than 10–14 days
* Cough lasts more than a week
* There is ear pain, persistent fussiness or crying
* Temperature goes over 102˚F

Cough

KEY SYMPTOMS

Coughing, wheezing (often worse at night)

TREATMENT

* For children over age 6, pediatric cough medicine
* Extra fluids
* Cool-mist humidifier or vaporizer in room at night

CALL A DOCTOR IF...

* Coughing makes it difficult for your child to breathe easily; is painful and persistent and is accompanied by whooping, vomiting or turning blue; interferes with eating and sleeping; appears suddenly with a high fever

Cuts and Scrapes

KEY SYMPTOMS

Some bleeding, scraped or lacerated skin

TREATMENT

* Rinse with cool water to flush away debris
* Wash gently with warm water and soap
* Use a butterfly bandage to help close the wound
* For large, oozing scrapes: Treat with an antibiotic ointment, cover with a sterile bandage or gauze
* For a deeper cut or laceration: Apply pressure with clean gauze or cloth for 5–10 minutes; try not to stop to peek at wound, which would interrupt this pressure. Avoid using iodine

CALL A DOCTOR IF...

* The cut or laceration is more than $1/2$ inch long or is deep
* You can't get the wound clean, or you see pus, increased tenderness or redness around the site
* Fever develops

Earache

KEY SYMPTOMS

Pain in ear (babies may cry during feedings or pull on ear), fever, sometimes pus or fluid, difficulty hearing and/or sleeping

TREATMENT

* Pediatric acetaminophen or ibuprofen (for a child over 6 months)
* Place warm compress or heating pad on child's ear (for a child over 6 months)

CALL A DOCTOR IF...

* You child has a high fever
* Symptoms last more than 1-2 days or worsen

Tummy Ache

KEY SYMPTOMS

Constipation, diarrhea, stomach pain. A young baby may show these symptoms by crying, pulling up her legs, passing gas, vomiting or burping excessively

TREATMENT

* For constipation: Drink small amounts of water or prune juice (under 6 months), eat fruits and high-fiber foods (over 6 months)
* For diarrhea: Most cases are caused by viral intestinal infections that don't respond to medication. Probiotics may help mild diarrhea with vomiting. Use a pediatric electrolyte solution in place of normal diet. For significant diarrhea, withhold solid food and avoid liquids high in sugar; offer a pediatric electrolyte solution

CALL A DOCTOR IF...

* Your child has severe abdominal pain lasting more than an hour or two, with nausea, vomiting, loss of appetite

and fever (possibly appendicitis)

* Your baby has symptoms of dehydration: fewer wet diapers, no tears, or sunken eyes or fontanel (soft spot on head)
* Fever lasts longer than 24–48 hours
* There's bloody stool
* Vomiting lasts longer than 12–24 hours and/or vomit is green, blood-tinged or looks like coffee grounds
* Abdomen feels hard, is swollen or distended

* Child refuses to eat or drink and/or reports severe abdominal pain
* There is a rash or jaundice
* Your baby has excessive or a bright-green spit-up, it contains blood, she's very uncomfortable or crying very hard, spitting up is forceful (it shoots across the room)
* Diarrhea contains blood or excessive mucus; child has more than eight stools per day
* Symptoms aren't improving with time

Emergency Alert

Here's when to take your child to the ER right away.

- Difficulty breathing
- Severe allergic reaction (shortness of breath, lip/oral swelling, persistent vomiting, altered mental status)
- High fever with headache and stiff neck
- Sudden difficulty in waking
- Sudden loss of sight, speech or movement
- Broken bone pushing through the skin
- Body part near an injured bone that is numb, tingling, weak, cold or pale

- Heavy bleeding or deep wound
- Serious burn
- Coughing or throwing up blood
- Fast heartbeat that doesn't slow down
- Vomiting followed by dry mouth, not crying tears, no urination in more than eight hours, or acting very sleepy/ "out of it"
- Rectal temperature greater than 100.4°F in children less than 2 months of age

When to call 911:

- Choking
- Severe difficulty breathing
- Head injury and unconsciousness
- Injury to neck or spine
- Child is not breathing or has turned blue
- Severe burn
- Seizure lasting more than five minutes
- Bleeding that can't be stopped

Source: C.S. Mott Children's Hospital, University of Michigan

Coping With Developmental Disorders

Worried that your child isn't reaching all his milestones on time?
Addressing developmental delays early can help him get back on track.

Jennifer S. had a feeling something wasn't quite right with her infant son, Timothy. When she brought her face to his, his eyes rarely focused on hers. When she smiled at him, he seemed in a daze, never mirroring the upward curve of her lips or the joy in her eyes. Timothy was Jennifer's first child, and she was unsure whether her gut-level concerns–why does something just feel off?–were warranted.

With the help of her pediatrician, Jennifer had Timothy evaluated by a team of early-childhood experts, who found he was exhibiting a cognitive and social-emotional delay. At 2.5 years old, he was reevaluated and diagnosed with autism spectrum disorder. These were hard truths to swallow. But identifying her son's disability early meant he received treatment during a crucial stage of his development, improving his success at school and among peers.

Approximately one out of every six children in the U.S. is diagnosed with a developmental delay (the term used for cognitive, social, emotional or physical challenges prior to age 3) or developmental disability (the term used for such challenges from age 3 onward), according to the Centers for Disease Control and Prevention. And not all delays warrant a diagnosis. But left unaddressed, these delays may set a child up for increased challenges as they grow older.

Identifying a Problem

Discerning whether your child has a delay or is just taking a bit longer to reach a milestone can be tricky. But several red flags during your child's first years of life can be telling.

You probably have grounds to be concerned "if your infant isn't able to track objects with his eyes; hold her head up consistently when placed on her tummy; and isn't babbling, cooing or beginning to say words by age 1," explains Laurie Zelinger, PhD, a board-certified school psychologist. Not smiling by 6 months of age, resisting or reacting strongly to being soothed, and not showing interest in others or her surroundings are other signs that an infant may have a developmental delay or be at risk for a disability later in life.

By age 2, if your child is not pointing to things she wants, cannot stack blocks or is struggling to form basic sentences (like, "Want more juice") and follow simple instructions (think: "Bring Mommy the ball") she could be experiencing a cognitive delay, Zelinger adds. Equally indicative is if a child cannot engage in joint attention—looking to where a caregiver is looking, or looking to and from a caregiver and a toy while playing. Once age 3 rolls around, difficulties in walking, running and feeding

Where to Get Help

The following websites and organizations provide a wealth of knowledge and guidance for parents concerned about potential delays or disabilities.

✱ Autism Speaks offers comprehensive information about autism spectrum disorders in addition to advocacy and other support services. (autismspeaks.org)

✱ The Centers for Disease Control and Prevention The Developmental Disabilities homepage provides info about specific conditions, ongoing studies and resources for families (cdc.gov/ncbddd)

✱ The Department of Education boasts a comprehensive list of resources for families looking to learn more about developmental disabilities, as well as their rights under the IDEA act. (www2.ed.gov)

✱ Disability Rights Education & Defense Fund (DREDF) advocates on behalf of individuals with disabilities living in the U.S. (dredf.org)

1 in 6: the number of kids in the U.S. diagnosed with a developmental delay or disability

1 in 68: The number of children in the U.S. meeting the criteria for autism.

become reasons to worry, says Robert Goldman, PsyD, JD, supervising psychologist at The CIIT Medical Center in Plainview, New York. So do traits such as avoiding eye contact, being disinterested in peers or performing "stereotyped" behaviors (such as hand-flapping, swaying, spinning or rocking) at any age.

Hypersensitivity to touch or sound; difficulties sucking, swallowing or breathing; and extreme pickiness once solid foods become introduced can also be warning signs of a delay or disability, says Ari S. Yares, PhD, a nationally certified school psychologist in Potomac, Maryland.

If you notice any of the above signs, don't wait too long to contact your pediatrician, Goldman advises. Your doctor can screen your child for delays or disabilities and refer you to an early-intervention or special-education program that, per the Individuals with Disabilities Education Act (IDEA), must offer free evaluations and services for qualifying families. Each state also has Parent Training and Information Centers (PTIs), which provide parents with support and education related to disabilities as well as guidance on obtaining services. Do an internet search for your local PTI, to get started.

Getting Help

Research shows that many evidence-based treatments can help address developmental disorders and delays. Speech therapy helps children produce, articulate and better comprehend language–and can help with feeding issues, like chewing and swallowing. Physical and occupational therapy address gross and fine motor skills. And behavior therapies help reinforce desired behaviors (such as sharing, sitting still and making eye contact) and reduce troubling ones (like biting or hitting).

While most developmental disorders cannot be entirely resolved through treatment, addressing them early can reduce just how much of an impairment individuals may experience throughout their lives and improve their ability to function and be more independent at home, in school, at work and in social settings. Ideally, children should start treatment before beginning school. "Early intervention is especially important during children's first five years of life, when their brains are rapidly developing new connections and are at their most malleable," says Yares. "The data shows that getting kids support by preschool age or sooner has an impact on their learning and outcomes later in life."

Children diagnosed with autism spectrum disorder (ASD) can especially gain from early intervention. Applied behavior analysis (ABA) is the most common treatment for ASD. It entails planning and assessment of goals, ranging from basic communication skills (e.g., asking for a desired item) to emotion regulation (counting to 10 when angry instead of throwing or breaking objects). ABA therapists reward desired behaviors and ignore undesired ones. "Social-skills training and providing opportunities for children to engage with peers who don't have a diagnosis of autism have also been shown to help children with autism learn to model appropriate social behavior," adds Goldman.

Common Autism Myths

Autism spectrum disorder (ASD) refers to a range of impairments in cognitive, behavioral, communication and social-interaction abilities. Approximately one in every 68 children in the U.S. meets the criteria for autism. Although awareness about autism has increased in recent years, there are still many common misconceptions about the disorder. Here are a few of the biggest that advocates and professionals are working hard to dispel.

MYTH No. 1

Vaccines can cause autism. Numerous studies have disproved the false link between vaccines and autism popularized by a now discredited doctor in the late 1990s. Put simply: There is no connection between getting your child vaccinated and an increased risk of autism. And not vaccinating your child puts her at a much greater risk of getting seriously ill—one reason there has been a resurgence of infectious diseases—such as measles, mumps and whooping cough—throughout much of the U.S.

MYTH No. 2

Autism looks the same in every case. "Autism spectrum disorder is a complex collection of symptoms, and not every child exhibits every one," explains psychologist Ari Yares. "Children may receive a diagnosis range from high-functioning to low-functioning." Some may be incredibly gifted in a specific area— approximately one in every 10 cases of autism exhibits "savantism"— yet struggle to express empathy and connect with peers. Others may experience severe delays in learning, communication, emotion-regulation and self-help skills.

MYTH No. 3

People with autism don't feel empathy. Autism itself is not a barrier to empathy. Rather, a condition called alexithymia—which is more common among individuals with autism spectrum disorder—can make understanding and identifying emotions difficult. About half of all individuals with autism meet the criteria for alexithymia.

Make Time for Play

Today's kids are spending fewer hours outdoors —and less time overall in unstructured play. Here's why both of those experiences are key to your child's mind and body.

Few things shout "childhood" as clearly as the sight of kids chasing each other around a playground. But these days, that image is fading so quickly that some experts say our children are suffering from "nature deficit disorder"—a lack of outdoor time so extreme that it's affecting their cognitive and emotional development. Numerous studies have documented that children today spend much less time playing outdoors than the previous generation did;

one large study in preschool-age children in Seattle found that only half the children had even one parent-supervised outdoor play opportunity per day. It is now estimated that the average American child spends four to seven minutes a day in unstructured play outdoors, and over seven hours a day in front of a screen.

The reasons for this deficit abound: We have many more available screens, from tablets and computers to TVs and video games, which entice children to

Free play, with no rules beyond being creative and spontaneous, expands your child's imagination.

stay indoors (and many busy parents may welcome the "electronic babysitter"). There is more ambient fear and worry about children's safety outside the home (despite clear evidence that children are no more endangered today than they were decades ago). Another factor is a change in teaching, with more homework being assigned and more emphasis on standardized tests, leading many parents to think that time indoors studying is far more important to their child's future than getting more playtime outside.

But they couldn't be more wrong about that, according to Doris Fromberg, EdD, director of early childhood teacher education at Hofstra University in New York. "For young children, play is often a full-body activity that helps them develop skills they will need later in life," Fromberg said in a TED Talk. "Running, dancing, climbing, rolling–these activities all foster muscle development and help fine-tune motor skills. Children also build their mental and emotional muscles as they create elaborate, imaginative worlds rich with a system of rules that govern the terms of play."

In short, both playing and simply being outdoors are crucial to your child's overall development. And while they can certainly be combined–devising "make-believe" games while building a fort in the backyard–each activity brings its own specific benefits to your child. Here's a breakdown of both.

The Nature Connection

In the 1980s, a Harvard University biologist named Edward O. Wilson proposed a theory called biophilia: that humans are instinctively drawn toward their natural surroundings.

That certainly sounds intuitive in an evolutionary sense, since early man spent almost all his time outdoors, largely in a search for food and shelter. Here's what going outside does for children:

* Improves sensory awareness.
Nature activates the senses more powerfully than, say, a video game, according to Richard Louv, author of *Last Child in the Woods: Saving Our Children from Nature-Deficit Disorder.* "Outside, you can see, hear, smell and touch the environment. As the young spend less and less of their lives in natural surroundings, their senses narrow, and this reduces the richness of human experience." In a larger sense, Louv adds, being in nature spurs curiosity and wonder in children that can make them feel more connected. "The natural phenomena in backyards and parks make kids ask questions about the Earth and the life it supports," he says.

* Protects eyesight.
"In the early 1970s, 25 percent of Americans were nearsighted; now, it's up to 42 percent," says Sam Wang, PhD, associate professor of neuroscience at Princeton University. The apparent reason: We're spending much more time indoors under artificial lights. "Humans' brains and eyes originated long ago, when we spent most of our waking hours in the sun," he explains. "Researchers suspect that bright outdoor light helps children's developing eyes maintain the right distance between the lens and retina, which keeps vision in focus. Dim indoor lighting doesn't provide the same kind of feedback, so many children's eyes don't grow correctly." Even though myopia

Playtime is a chance to boost dexterity, emotional strength and imagination.

Kids who play outside tend to sleep better at night.

(nearsightedness) can be highly inheritable, a study at The Ohio State University found that, among children with two myopic parents, those who spent at least two hours per day outdoors were four times less likely to be nearsighted than those who spent less than one hour per day outside.

* Increases future happiness.

There is powerful evidence that when children spend lots of time outdoors, they are more likely to be happier and less anxious as adults. A recent long-term and large-scale study in Denmark quantified this effect, and found that children raised surrounded by nature had a 55 percent lower incidence of developing mental-health issues as adults–and that the more time spent outside, the better the mental-health outcome. Researchers speculate that the nature-happiness connection may be multipronged: Being outdoors more promotes physical health, which is associated with positive mood. Spending time in nature may help build self-reliance, resiliency and patience. And there may be something intrinsic in nature that is soothing to humans, making them feel part of a larger, connected world. Many mental-health programs that treat conditions like PTSD or anxiety use the outdoors as a tool or pathway.

The Power of Play

Surprisingly, the first real insights into the role of play in children's lives were advanced a century ago, by the Russian developmental psychologist Lev Vygotsky. His core theory was that child development is the result of interaction between children and their social environment–in short, that play spurs learning more powerfully than passively being exposed to "teaching." Here's what we have learned since then about what play does:

* Teaches self-regulation.

In other words, the ability to regulate their emotions and think before they act. Role-playing games are especially key to learning this all-important life skill, because out of necessity they put children into someone else's skin. And because unsupervised play allows kids to make their own decisions during the "game," it teaches them to begin making connections between their choices and the natural consequences of those choices. For instance, if you throw something, it might break. If you cut someone out of participating in your game, you may lose a friend. Self-regulation is what allows a child, as he gets older, to work toward longer-term goals, and also teaches him how to get along with others–a key social skill.

* Unites different cognitive areas and skills.

Unlike filling out worksheets or looking at screens, active and unregulated play "pulls together the logical and creative parts of the brain," says Fromberg. "Young children learn in very different ways than adults," she explains. "They learn by comparing physical experiences, by interactions with other people and their own feelings. And they learn an enormous amount through their imagination." It's a kind of whole-body and whole-mind experience that's quite foreign to the more regimented and focused way that older children and adults "study."

Many experts call children "little scientists," because every day they're conducting experiments in the world around them. The things they learn from those hands-on experiences are much more powerful than something they are simply told or read about.

✳ Promotes risk-taking and curiosity.
A curious child is a child driven to learn and soak up experience–great skills for her future intellectual and emotional development. And playing, alone or with others, fosters curiosity.

Since free play happens in an unpressured, open-ended environment, a child can try new things without fear of making a mistake or being embarrassed. "Risk-taking in children's play may be an important developmental process," says Wang. Because play unfolds in a relaxed environment, and allows brain signals to fire without being waylaid by stress, a child's brain is more able to explore possibilities and learn from them, says Wang. "In other words, a major function of play may well be to provide practice for real life."

Screen Time

Years ago the debate was simply about TV time. Now it's about: TV, video games, smartphones, tablets, social media, texting...there are so many screens—and it is so tempting for parents to quiet a child by handing her a device. But experts are concerned about the effect of screens on young minds. Here, some advice:

✳ Model good media use.
Don't bring the phone to dinner or check messages when you're with your child. Create media-free spaces at home, and never make kids compete with a screen for your attention.

✳ Don't make it a reward.
It's tempting to give out

screen time as a "bribe," but that makes it more desirable and compelling.

✳ Leave the tablet at home.
It's key to your child's development for them to look around and learn to find entertainment and interest in their surroundings. Also, don't let screens be part of playdates.

✳ Avoid screens for the first two years. The American Academy of Pediatrics advises one hour—tops—of high-quality programming a day from ages 2 to 5.

✳ Share your thoughts.
As your children grow, you should continue to

share viewing so you can discuss some of the media messages (like gender roles). This also teaches them to watch TV and movies actively, not passively, which develops self-esteem.

Kids and Meditation

Little minds can reap big benefits from mindfulness,
from enhanced learning to better focus.
Here's why children take to it so easily, and how you can help.

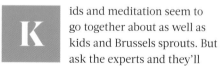ids and meditation seem to go together about as well as kids and Brussels sprouts. But ask the experts and they'll tell you that children may actually have a knack for it. "I definitely think they're more in the present moment than adults, so they have a natural inclination to notice what's happening and be aware," says Stephanie Romero, EdD, executive director and founder of Awaken Pittsburgh, a nonprofit that teaches mindfulness practices.

While research into kids and meditation is still emerging, early trials suggest it can yield serious benefits. In one 2016 study, published in the journal *Pediatrics*, 300 children in two lower-income Baltimore schools were randomly assigned to mindfulness-based stress reduction (aka MBSR, a specific type of mindfulness

Apps: Pro or Con?

There's an app for everything—and kids' meditation is no exception. "Young people are on their devices, and maybe taking advantage of that to support practicing is good," says Stephanie Romero, EdD, executive director and founder of Awaken Pittsburgh. "However, there's no substitute for human connection and one-on-one support." Research out of the University of Otago, New Zealand, shows that mindfulness apps can improve people's mental health. Give them a try and see if they appear to be helping or hurting your child's practice and concentration.

practice) or health-education classes for 12 weeks. At the end of the trial, those who'd followed the MBSR program were significantly less likely to have depression, self-hostility, rumination and other signs of distress. In another study, published in the *Journal of Adolescent Health* in 2011, researchers randomly assigned 166 adolescents at increased risk of cardiovascular disease to a three-month program of breathing awareness meditation (BAM), life-skills training, or health education. Those who participated in BAM had a reduction in heart rate and blood pressure.

The evidence in favor of meditation is strong enough that the American Academy of Pediatrics (AAP) encourages pediatricians to have an open dialogue with their patients about their use of meditation and other so-called "complementary" therapies, saying these appear to be safe and potentially effective in controlling pain and anxiety, among other chronic conditions.

Programs for Tiny Meditators

The AAP isn't alone in recognizing meditation's upsides for kids: Various schools and other institutions have embraced it. Newark Yoga Movement, for instance, is a 10-year-old nonprofit that's brought mindfulness and yoga to 32,000 children in the Newark, New Jersey, school system. "We teach meditation, but we never call it that. At the end of many of our yoga classes we do 'quiet breathing.' We can show the students how—through one minute of breathing—they can chill out," says Debby Kaminsky, e-RYT, Newark Yoga Movement's founder.

Romero's Awaken Pittsburgh currently operates in local Brashear High School and has also trained teachers from 12 other schools. Instructors lead students through

Meditation gives children the skills to help soothe themselves.

What's in a name? Many in-school programs avoid using the words "meditation" or "yoga" since they potentially have religious connotations that may be off-putting for some families or school officials.

a different mind-body practice each week. Exercises might involve picking an object to focus on, and then consciously bringing their attention back to it as the mind wanders. "We might also have them imagine something they regret doing, then forgiving themselves for that," says Romero.

In Chicago, the Namaste Charter School fully embraces meditation as part of its curriculum. "I've been floored by walking into PE classes and seeing kindergartners sitting and meditating," says executive director Natalie Neris.

Colorado Children's Hospital in Aurora utilizes meditation in its outpatient therapy for kids with anxiety issues. "The most basic meditation I lead kids through is to inhale and exhale, and to focus on their exhale," says group leader and yoga therapist Michelle Fury, LPC, C-IAYT. Among other exercises, Fury also leads her young patients in walking meditation, where they have to be mindful of using their bodies while connecting with the environment.

Do Try This at Home

Wynne Kinder, MEd, who teaches kids in the urban school districts in Lancaster, Pennsylvania, through her Wellness Works in Schools program, sees a real change in her students. "I think the benefits are far-reaching, from enhanced academic ability to noticing when they are distracted," she says.

If you're eager to see some of these same changes in your own child, there are plenty of meditation exercises you can do together.

One tension-reliever that Kinder, author of the book *Calm: Mindfulness for Kids*, recommends children of just about any age do is called "melting": Together with your child, stand with your arms crossed, holding your shoulders with your hands. Tuck your chin and tighten (or "freeze") every muscle of your body, starting with your feet and moving up. After holding that position for a few seconds, start to loosen (or "melt"), from the top down, letting your arms glide down to your sides and your legs bend as you sink to the floor in an imaginary puddle. Repeat once or twice.

Kelsey Evans, e-RYT, a kids' yoga instructor and host of the *Happy Healthy Kids* show on PBS, is a fan of what she calls Chocolate Meditation. "I hand a Hershey's kiss to the child and ask them to examine it and slowly unwrap it, listening to the crinkling of the foil. They smell it, observe it, and then slowly put it in their mouth, placing it on the tip of their tongue and holding it there for a couple of seconds before slowly eating it." It helps kids learn to concentrate and become more aware of their senses.

If you'd like to keep it ultra simple, try Fury's recommendation: "Set a timer for five minutes–choose a gentle alarm sound– and say to your child, 'Pay attention to your breaths going in and out, and think of something that makes you happy. When you feel your mind wandering, bring it back to the thing that makes you happy.'" Join in on the exercise; you'll both benefit from the focused quiet time.

Walk the Walk

It's great to teach your kids to be more mindful. But being a more mindful parent is just as important, says Nadia Sabri, MD, founder of The Mindful MD Mom blog. "Mindful parenting empowers mothers and fathers to recognize their role as facilitators to help their kids thrive in their environment, and parenting becomes a loving team approach between the adults and the kids," explains Sabri. Some tips she recommends:

1 Be aware of your own triggers. Parenthood can make our childhood and past experiences resurface. By consciously acknowledging our beliefs and limitations, we can respond, instead of react, to even the most frustrating situations.

2 Practice mindful breathing. Inhale through the nose and slowly exhale through the mouth. This lowers your heart rate and stress levels, giving a feeling of calm.

3 Model the behavior you want. "Kids observe the world around them and respond to the nonverbal cues, like facial expressions and tone and volume of voice," Sabri says. "This is one of the main reasons that yelling at kids really does not work." Instead, get down at their eye level, speak softly and model the desired behavior.

4 Apologize when you mess up. You can't model negative behavior and expect perfection from your kids, says Sabri.

5 Recognize when you're nearing your limits. Even on busy days, try to find some time for self-care, so you don't reach the point of parental burnout.

Snuggle Up!

Who doesn't love a good cuddle or well-timed hug? But the benefits to your child go far beyond the momentary pleasure.

Hugs come naturally. When a child is hurt or distressed, we hug to comfort them. When they're tired, we settle them on our laps to promote a nap. And when we're happy or playing with a child, we hug just for fun. It's a no-brainer.

But science is showing that the power of those touches is much greater than it may seem in the moment, and goes far deeper in children's psyches. Touch is, in fact, central to development and psychological stability–and that connection begins at birth.

"There is some interesting work showing that in mothers who have just given birth, the skin area on their chest is a degree or two higher than the rest of their body–it's like a natural warming area for the newborn," says Ann Bigelow, PhD, a professor and researcher of developmental psychology at St. Francis Xavier University in Antigonish, Nova Scotia. "The mother can thermoregulate for the baby, so if the baby's temperature drops, the mother's rises, and vice versa." Beyond that first, and basic, application of warmth, a childhood full of touch and hugging is key to a child's health and development, thanks to chemical messengers from the hypothalamus. Here are some of the things snuggling can do.

Hugs Encourage Trust and Bonding

Trust is at the heart of most human interactions, binding us together and allowing us to move forward developmentally. Without trust, humans are afraid to take risks in order to develop into a fully rounded person. Close touch triggers the release of oxytocin, the "love hormone," which has been shown to increase trust in others and, perhaps most importantly, encourage healthy attachment between the child and his or her primary caregivers.

Hugs help kids grow. Beyond its emotional effects, oxytocin also has a physical effect:

It has been shown to increase the amount of growth factor (IGF-1) in the blood. That promotes growth in general, but it also helps speed healing–so yes, that skinned knee really will feel better sooner!

Hugs Encourage Long-Term Relationships

Oxytocin has a partner hormone, vasopressin, which is also released through loving touch. Vasopressin has been specifically linked to the development of long-term, committed relationships, because it helps mediate fear and mistrust.

Hugs Reduce Stress

Researchers have studied children who were adopted after spending their infancy in Eastern European orphanages, where there was very limited physical contact between caregivers and babies (even the bottles were propped up rather than held by a caregiver). When the children were adopted by American families, they had higher levels of the stress hormone cortisol–even after several years of living in a stable and loving home. Prolonged exposure to cortisol has been shown to compromise a child's immune system and affect memory and verbal reasoning later in life.

Hugs Produce Resilient Children

Psychological resources like optimism and self-esteem can buffer against stress and predict a healthier, more tenacious person. Scientists recently found a link between those resources and oxytocin: People who scored high in them had a certain type of oxytocin receptor in their DNA; those scoring lower, who were more depression-prone, had a different receptor. This confirmed that oxytocin is a key mediator for happiness and self-esteem–so the more of it your child receives through hugs, the better.

✕

Love It!
The more you hug,
the healthier
your child.

93

What Pediatricians Really Wish Parents Would Do

There's a lot to learn about bringing up a child, but there might be a few things you may not have thought about. Consider the following advice from top kids' docs.

1 Ditch the Bottle Early

The American Academy of Pediatrics recommends that you stop giving your baby a bottle around his first birthday, and no later than 18 months. That's in part to help him start to learn new skills, but also because prolonged bottle use can add excess calories to the diet. One recent study found that 22 percent of babies were still given bottles regularly by the time they were 2–and nearly a quarter of them were obese before age 6. "Parents often have a hard time letting go of the baby years, and the bottle is an extension of that," says Sharon Somekh, MD, a pediatrician based in Roslyn, New York, and the founder of parenting website Raiseology. "But holding on to something too long can be unhealthy too."

2 Don't Panic if You See a Tick

Lyme disease can be scary, but your child's not destined to get sick if he picks up a tick or two. "If you live in an endemic area, it's important to do regular tick checks and remove a tick as soon as possible if you see one," says Gail Shust, MD, an assistant professor of pediatric infectious diseases at NYU Langone in New York City. If a critter has latched on, don't freak out. "Just because you've had contact with a tick does not mean you'll get Lyme disease," says Shust. "And if you do, the vast majority of people are cured with antibiotics."

3 Let Them Get Dirty

It's actually good for your kid to be messy sometimes. Scientists theorize that disinfecting every inch of our environment may ultimately make kids

✕
Kids as young as 6 months should get a yearly flu shot to reduce their chances of getting this potentially dangerous ailment.

Don't stress out at the office—when you stay calm, your child stays happy.

sicker. This "hygiene hypothesis" holds that if your home or your child is "too clean," her immune system may not be effectively challenged to respond to threats, increasing the risk of asthma and other immune-related conditions. Research also shows that newborns who live in a home with a dog are much less likely to develop allergies than those who do not share quarters with a pooch. "That doesn't mean you skip washing hands before you eat or after you go to the bathroom–but you can let your kid get a little down and dirty sometimes," says Somekh.

4 Be a Good Role Model

If your palms begin to sweat the moment you sign in at the pediatrician's office, do your best to calm down. "Parents are often just as anxious as their children when they come to an appointment, and kids pick up on that very easily," notes Somekh. Can't kick your anxiety to the curb? Fake it, especially when your child is scheduled to be vaccinated. "Your child is going to be much more likely to cry or carry on when you make a big deal over something like a shot," she adds. Tell her it will be fine and promise to do something special, like checking out a new playground, when it's all over.

5 Make Time to Play

It can be hard to find a minute to just have some fun. But playing with your kids does more than just burn off extra energy–it's an important part of their development. "Our kids spend so much of their days sitting in a car or in front of screen, but they really need some time every day to just run around, laugh and have fun," says Tanya Altmann, MD, a spokeswoman for the

American Academy of Pediatrics (AAP). And it's not just the little ones who can benefit from an epic freeze-tag battle. "Everyone's brain needs time to decompress," adds Altmann. "We just don't give ourselves time to unwind." So go ahead. Build that human pyramid, toss a ball in the backyard, have a tickle fight–whatever it takes to have fun.

6 Give Your Teen a Bedtime

You may have strictly enforced light's-out when your child was a toddler, but by high school, parents often hit the sack before their teens do. "Even adolescents need to go to bed at a regular time each night," notes Somekh. "Teens' days are packed from the moment they wake up until bed, and they often don't get a break." Teens need about eight to 10 hours of sleep to function at their best, but only a small percentage reach this goal on school nights. Make sure they hit the sack early–and keep devices like phones and computers out of the bedroom.

7 Keep Antibiotic Use to a Minimum

Many parents have gotten the message that taking too many antibiotics can do far more harm than good, says Altmann. Still, when your kid is complaining about an ear infection or an achy throat, it's only natural to hope you can get medication that will make it go away fast. "We need to keep in mind that most of the time when a child gets sick, it's caused by a virus," she notes. (Antibiotics treat bacterial infections, not viral infections.) Take antibiotics unnecessarily, and you risk that the next time your child really needs the medication, it won't be as effective. Instead, ask your doctor about natural therapies that may provide relief for things like a sore throat or a cold, such as nasal saline solutions, putting a humidifier in the bedroom and making sure your kids get plenty of fresh fruits and vegetables, fluids–and sleep.

8   Don't Ask Dr. Google

The internet is a wonderful tool, but sometimes having too much information can be a dangerous thing. "There's a lot of misleading information out there," notes Altmann. "Often parents can become pointed in the wrong direction or get misinformation that can lead to problems or cause extra stress." If in doubt, call your pediatrician– that's what she's there for.

9   Share Your Health-Care News

Urgent-care facilities have become a $15 billion-plus industry, with more than 10,000 facilities opening their doors by the end of 2019, according to medical market research firm Kalorama Information. And while they offer a huge convenience to busy families when it comes to checking out everything from sore throats to twisted ankles, it's important to keep your pediatrician informed about what's going on in terms of your child's health. "There are many benefits to urgent-care facilities, but they can sometimes fragment the health-care system," says Altmann. "If we don't get all the information about medications your child is taking or issues they may be having, things can be missed or fall through the cracks."

10   Get Your Child Vaccinated

"This includes the flu shot, too,"says Shust. "Even in seasons where the vaccine is not as effective as we would hope, it can still have some benefit in shortening the course of illness and lessening the intensity of disease if you or your child do get sick." The Centers for Disease Control and Prevention recommend that everyone 6 months of age or older get vaccinated each year against influenza.

Regular checkups keep your little ones on track.

CHAPTER 3

Growth and Development

Year by year, we all want our kids to grow to be their very best. Here's what to expect along the way, and how to help them at every age.

GROWING UP

INFANTS TO TODDLERS

age 0–2 years

The Crucial Period

During the first few years, a child goes through more rapid transformations than at any other time of life.

W e are all so familiar with how a baby grows–from unfocused infant to laughing 8-month-old to running, babbling toddler–that it's easy to gloss over the awe-inspiring construction job that's going on in her brain. For example, a study from the University of California, Berkeley, found that children's brains must store 1.5 megabytes of information in order to master their native language. In the first year of life, the cerebellum, center of movement and perception, triples in size. And by age 3, a child's brain has 80 percent of the volume it will have as an adult.

While much of this growth is hardwired and genetically programmed, research over the past 30 years has been demonstrating the profound interplay between genes and a baby's environment. Genetic predispositions can go either way, depending on how a child is nurtured and stimulated. "Children's early experiences shape their whole life trajectories," says

The average weight of a 1–month–old baby is 10 pounds.

Martha Farah, PhD, a neuroscientist and a professor of psychology at the University of Pennsylvania. "What scientists are beginning to unravel are the mechanisms by which these changes happen."

One thing we know is that a young child's caretaker plays an outsize role, says Gail Gross, PhD, EdD, MEd, author of *How to Build Your Baby's Brain*. "Any connection you make with your baby is making a connection in your baby's brain. His brain is crackling and popping with synapses with each encounter, building pathways for learning." Understanding how that works will help you promote not only his future cognitive abilities but also a stable emotional makeup.

In the Beginning

The story starts with neurons–the brain cells that process information and send it elsewhere in the brain and body. At birth, an infant has just about as many neurons as she ever will, about 100 billion of them. It's as if the brain's scaffolding is in place, but it needs wiring to connect everything. The wiring is supplied by synapses, which are junctions between neurons that enable signals to be passed along to other parts of the brain and body. A baby starts making synapses before birth, but their growth really explodes in the first three years, with 40,000 new synapses being added every second. It's like the baby's brain is in overdrive, making more synapses than she'll need–about twice as many as she will have as an adult.

The job of the learning baby, then, becomes cutting back on synapses, as the brain figures out which ones matter. "It's called pruning," says Gross. "The growing brain is very efficient, so it constantly dumps synapses

that aren't being utilized–kind of 'use it or lose it.'" Your baby's brain is prioritizing, based on his environment: figuring out which connections are important. Synapses that aren't being fired up are dumped, and synapses that are being tapped get stronger, Gross explains.

"Take learning a language," she says. "If the baby's mother speaks English, neurons gather into clusters and create a pathway that's specifically for English. If the baby is also hearing another language before the age of about 5, a pathway gets laid down for that as well. It's a window of development, and if a child learns a second language by 5 or so, she will speak it without an accent. By age 10, that window is fully closed, and if she learns a new language she'll speak it like a non-native speaker."

Like Clockwork

While a baby's brain is pruning to adapt to her environment, creating a unique human being that is a mix of genetics and experience, there are growth spurts that are shared by all infants. In the first year of life, for example, the explosive growth in the cerebellum, the area related to movement, is tied to the acquisition of motor skills. In 12 months a child learns to grasp and manipulate objects, roll over, sit up, crawl–and sometimes is walking by his first birthday. Meanwhile, the visual areas of the cortex develop, and an infant's initially dim and limited sight blossoms into full binocular vision.

In the second year, the greatest growth is in the parts of the brain dealing with language, leading to what researchers call a "vocabulary explosion." It's common for a child's vocabulary to quadruple between the

DEVELOPMENT MILESTONES

AGE: 0-1 MONTH

✳ Head lags behind when pulled up to sit ✳ Turns head to the side ✳ Able to follow objects to midline (1 month) ✳ Keeps hands tightly closed ✳ Holds objects placed in palm ✳ Regards faces

AGE: 2-4 MONTHS

✳ Raises head and chest when lying on tummy ✳ Follows objects past the midline with eyes ✳ Coos ✳ First smiles ✳ Recognizes parents ✳ Swipes at dangling objects ✳ Opens and shuts hands; grasps and shakes hand toys ✳ Anticipates feeding

AGE: 4-7 MONTHS

✳ Starts to roll from front to back and back to front ✳ Sits with, and then without, support of hands ✳ Transfers objects from hand to hand ✳ Grasps objects and brings them to mouth ✳ Develops full-color vision and ability to track moving objects ✳ Laughs; responds to voice ✳ Finds partially hidden objects

AGE: 8-12 MONTHS

✳ Gets to sitting position without help ✳ Crawls forward on belly ✳ Pulls self up to stand ✳ Walking holding on to furniture or hands; may walk 2 or 3 steps without support ✳ Puts objects in/takes them out of container ✳ Babbles; says words like "dada," "mama" and "uh oh!" ✳ Imitates gestures; begins to use objects (drinking from cup, brushing hair) ✳ Shy or anxious with strangers ✳ Finger-feeds himself ✳ Shows preferences for certain people and toys

AGE: 12-18 MONTHS

✳ Stands without help; takes steps with help; begins to walk alone and may even run ✳ Lets go of objects deliberately, attempts to scribble ✳ Imitates, responds when called ✳ Crawls up stairs ✳ Scribbles with pencils ✳ Says 4 to 6 words at a time; may have a vocabulary of 10 words or more ✳ Picks up and eats small pieces of food; uses spoon and cup without help ✳ Follows single- or two-step commands ✳ May develop separation anxiety

AGE: 18-24 MONTHS

✳ Starts to run ✳ Turns pages; scribbles spontaneously; imitates lines when drawing ✳ Throws and kicks a ball ✳ Climbs up and down steps without help ✳ Learns 1 or more words a week; uses sentences of 4 or 5 words ✳ Points to body parts; imitates tasks ✳ Finds object hidden under a few covers ✳ Begins make-believe play ✳ Starts to sort objects into groups ✳ Completes puzzles that have 3 or 4 pieces ✳ Learns to eat by herself ✳ May show signs of being ready for potty training

From infancy to toddlerhood, these are busy days (and nights!) as your child learns and grows.

first and second birthday. By the third year, the prefrontal cortex reaches peak synaptic density. This is when children develop more complex cognitive abilities, understanding cause and effect and using the past to interpret present events.

Certain leaps forward in cognition happen on an amazingly precise timeline. Alison Gopnik, PhD, a professor of psychology at the University of California, Berkeley, and author of *Philosophical Baby*, describes one of these: the ability to take the perspective of another person. "It's a very profound ability. It's at the root of a lot of our social and moral lives," she says. An experiment with goldfish crackers and broccoli shows how it works. Since all babies prefer goldfish to broccoli, the experimenter would pretend to like broccoli (taking a piece and saying, "Mmmm, I love broccoli!") and to not like the crackers ("Yuck, crackers!"). Then she'd put her hand between the bowls and say, "Can you give me some?" And although the babies preferred the goldfish crackers, they would hand her broccoli. It worked the other way, too: If the experimenter said she liked the crackers better, the babies would hand her those.

"This was with 18-month-old babies," says Gopnik. "They already understood that someone else might have a different preference than they did—and they also had the impulse to give someone what the person wanted rather than what they themselves wanted." The other startling thing, Gopnik adds, is that 15-month-old babies didn't do this. Instead, they always gave the experimenter what they themselves liked: crackers. "So this isn't something that's there from the get-go. It's not there innately. It seems to be something babies learn between 15 and 18 months. They're figuring out, 'Oh, I see, people don't always want the same thing.'"

Fast Facts

* Most babies grow rapidly in their first six weeks, gaining an average weight of ¾ ounce per day.
* The bones in your baby's skull are still growing together even after she's born. The skull grows faster during the first four months than at any other time in a baby's life.
* Balding baby? The fine hair that may have covered your child's head when he was born often begins to fall out in his first week or so.
* The umbilical cord stump should fall off within the first 10 to 21 days after birth.

Even very young kids love looking at books.

Reflex Action

Babies are born with a variety of reflexes that are ways of protecting themselves:

MORO REFLEX This occurs when your baby's head shifts or falls back or if she is startled: She may react by throwing out her arms and legs and extending her neck, then bringing her arms together.

TONIC NECK REFLEX When his head turns to one side, the arm on that side straightens; the opposite arm bends.

GRASP REFLEX Stroke the palm of his hand, and he'll grip your finger.

WALKING/STEPPING Hold her under your arms (support her head) and let her soles touch a flat surface. She will place one foot in front of the other.

ROOTING Turning her head toward your hand if you stroke her cheek or mouth helps her find the nipple when it's time to eat.

Little Scientists

The goldfish experiment also shows how babies' brains gradually integrate their own experience into a growing knowledge base. "A lot of what babies and young children are doing is like what scientists are doing," says Gopnik. "When they play at 'pretend,' it's like a scientific thought experiment, figuring out how people work." And playing with wooden blocks—learning that a heavy one on top will make a tower tumble—is teaching them about physics. What parents should know, Gopnik adds, is that "all of this learning takes place in a protected, nurturing context. This period is when children are free to learn and explore without having to put that learning to work, and you need a good caretaker in order to be that free and creative."

Your child's brain is wired for discovery, says Gross. "A securely bonded child will test the limitations of the environment." Your job is to make that environment as rich as possible. One thing Gross advocates is using music, especially the slow "largo" or "adagio" movements of Baroque music, which are in sync with the rhythm of the heart. "Neuroscience researchers have measured how music enhances not only the function of your brain, but also its form. Brain scans show, for example, that music bridges the right and left hemispheres of the brain." And you don't have to buy complicated "learning toys." All a young child needs is right in your home, and is more stimulating to the imagination.

"Anything your child can classify, sort, number or order can become an intellectual activity," says Gross. "Plastic bowls and lids, fabrics or buttons can all be sorted by size, texture, color or shape." The bottom line, says Gopnik: Kids are always more imaginative than toy makers, so give them the tools to help them grow.

Babies form secure attachments soon after birth.

When to Worry

Wondering if your child is on track? How to tell.

Most babies and toddlers reach certain language milestones at predictable times, but sometimes a hearing or speech problem gets in the way. The American Speech-Language-Hearing Association advises parents to consult a specialist if your child misses these marks:

☐ Not smiling or playing with others from birth to 3 months.

☐ Making few sounds and very few gestures, such as pointing, by 7 to 12 months.

☐ Not understanding what other people are saying, from 7 months to 2 years.

☐ A lack of interest in playing or talking with other children at 2 to 3 years.

☐ A lack of interest in books or drawing by age 2½ to 3 years.

TODDLERS TO PRESCHOOL
age 2-4 years

The Trouble With Transitions

Sometimes a toddler is harder to move than a 2-ton boulder. Here's why—and what to do about it.

What is it about getting from the door of the house to the car, or from playtime to bath time, that is so challenging when it involves a 3-year-old? Nobody loves transitions, but young children seem to loathe them most of all. Perhaps it's the power struggle, some experts propose: In the 2- to 5-year group, kids are working toward independence, which makes them chafe at any and all limits and authority over them.

There are other, more subtle, reasons as well, say child-development researchers. "Young children are especially vulnerable to transitions, transferring from one activity to another or one place to another, simply

DEVELOPMENT MILESTONES

AROUND AGE 2

* Climbs well * Walks up and down stairs, alternating feet * Kicks a ball * Runs easily * Pedals tricycle * Holds a pencil in a writing position; makes vertical, horizontal or circular strokes with a pencil or crayon * Follows two- or three-part commands * Uses pronouns (I, you, me, we, they) * Sorts objects by shape and color * Plays make-believe * Understands concepts of "mine," "yours," "his/hers"

AROUND AGE 3

* Hops on one foot for up to five seconds; moves forward and back * Goes up and down stairs without help * Kicks ball; throws ball overhand; catches bounced ball * Can draw a person with two or more body parts * Uses scissors; draws circles and squares * Masters basic rules of grammar * Correctly names colors; may know numbers and count * Engages in fantasy play * Negotiates conflicts

AROUND AGE 4

* Stands on one foot for 10 seconds or longer * Hops, somersaults, swings and climbs; may skip * Tells stories, uses future tense * Can count 10 or more objects; names at least four colors * Understands time * Draws full person, prints some letters * Dresses without help * Copies triangles and other geometric shapes * Uses fork, spoon and knife * Uses bathroom on own * Distinguishes fantasy from reality

because of their immaturity," says Gail Gross, PhD, EdD. "They dislike change." Anxious or timid children in particular may be sensitive to transitions because they're fearful of the new situation they will be required to confront. And one thing to note about transitions of all kinds, says David Anderson, MD, senior director of the ADHD and Behavior Disorders Center at the Child Mind Institute, is that "often we are transitioning from a preferred activity–something we like doing–to something that we need to do."

Adults can relate to that, but at least we've had decades to hone our coping mechanisms and emotional self-control. When it comes to your whining or intransigent toddler, the experts have some advice.

Prepare Your Child

No one likes to be unceremoniously yanked away from what they're doing–not even grown-ups. So start planting the seed before you're ready to move on or change activities, says Gross. "Say, 'In a little while we're going to....' Give him time to adjust to the upcoming change." You could also institute not only a "preview" but a countdown, says Michael Rosenthal, PhD, a pediatric neuropsychologist. Before each transition, give a time frame for what will happen, along with countdowns–in 20 minutes, then 10, then five, it will be time to finish breakfast and go to preschool. "This allows your child to emotionally get ready for an event." You could try using a timer so you both have a visual cue for how much time is left before the transition happens.

Create Routines

Many young children are thrown off by transitions because they're more comfortable with consistency, routines and structure–so start building a predictable structure for your child, as much as possible.

Potty Time

Most kids can start to be potty trained between 2 and 3 years old, although it very much depends on your child. Here are some ways to get started.

Make sure he's ready.
Signs include: staying dry for several hours at a time; having regular bowel movements about the same time each day; asking to be changed when his diaper is dirty and/or showing signs he's about to go (like squatting). He may also ask to use the toilet. "To be truly toilet trained, your toddler has to be able to sense that he needs to go, be able to interpret that sensation and then be able to tell you and take action (get the pee or poop into the potty)," writes Tanya Altmann, MD, in *Baby & Toddler Basics*.

Get the lingo down.
Start "potty talk" early, advises Altmann. Teach your child words you feel comfortable with her using (pee, poop, wee-wee, doody...).

Lead by example.
Announce when you have to go to the bathroom, and—if you're comfortable doing so—let her watch you use the toilet. And show how you always wash your hands after you go.

Make it fun.
Read a story, sing a song, tell some jokes. "Try not to scold or force him to sit there if he can't go—it works much better if you praise his efforts, however small they are," notes Altmann. Positive reinforcement is key. You might also want to give rewards like stickers, stamps or small treats.

Wash, wash, wash.
Start the lifelong habit of always washing hands after you use the bathroom. Keep soap and towels within reach and give her a small step stool to reach the sink. Teach your child to sing a song ("Happy Birthday" works well) so he gets a feel for how long it should take to scrub his hands (do it for at least 20 seconds).

Night and day.
Remember that potty training mostly centers around using the toilet during the daytime. Don't be surprised that your child will likely continue to need pull-ups or a diaper at night. And don't worry about bed-wetting or admonish your child, says Altmann: "Accidents happen."

All kids potty train at their own pace.

For example, even though a bedtime routine might seem like something that's only for babies, toddlers and preschoolers (and beyond!) benefit from having a clear progression toward lights-out. You could follow a pattern like dinner, bath, some quiet playtime or reading time, then snuggle and kiss goodnight. The same holds for a morning routine, especially on school days. Take regularly scheduled steps toward leaving the house to prepare your child for the transition to school.

Surviving the Terrible Twos

Around age 2, kids may start expressing frustration as they become more independent. To make it through:

Ignore it. Usually, kids throw tantrums to get attention—so don't give in. Walk away or don't react.

Channel her energy. When she starts to get worked up, turn her attention to a new activity or do something new yourself, like reading a book.

Give a time-out. Pick a location where your child must sit or stand —no more than one minute per year of age— until he calms down.

Praise the good. When your child is behaving well, reward her by giving stickers or playing a new game.

Just leave. If you're in public, like the grocery store or a restaurant, take your child outside until he calms down.

Don't Cave

Your toddler is a genius when it comes to figuring out which of your buttons to push. So when an upcoming transition triggers a tantrum, meltdown or insistent whining, she will check out how you respond. If you give in to "five more minutes" after you've set a deadline, she'll know that at least some of the time her stratagems can work. That guarantees even more of a meltdown at the next transition, so set up the schedule and then stick to your guns!

Get Their Attention

Make a direct connection when you're leading up to a transition, says Matthew Rouse, PhD, MSW, a clinical psychologist at the Child Mind Institute. This could mean eye contact, sitting down next to them, putting a hand on their shoulder or asking them to repeat back to you what you've just said. What doesn't work: yelling instructions to them from the next room and assuming your message has gotten through—or even has been heard at all.

Praise Every Good Transition

There's really nothing stronger than positive feedback when you're trying to establish good patterns with your child. "For all the times a transition has gone wrong," says Rouse, "there have probably been a lot more times when it's gone right. Don't lose those opportunities to be really enthusiastic and say this was so great, it went so smoothly, I really liked how you handed over the iPad right away and started brushing your teeth, and now we have more time to read." The more specific you can be in your praise, the more effective it will be. You are showing your child clearly what kind of behaviors work—and will get them extra parental attention, which is what every child craves.

At about age 2, most children engage in parallel play.

Picky eater?
Don't give up
too soon.

Turn Yuk...Into Yum!

Face it: Most kids aren't born with a love of broccoli or lima beans, but experts say everyone can develop a taste for healthy chow.

Hiding nutritious ingredients—such as fruits, veggies, whole grains, legumes and yogurt—in your kids' favorite foods is just one strategy to get them to eat healthy foods. The ultimate goal, of course, is to get them to truly crave those healthy foods. Here are a few tips to grow a good eater.

Start early.
When you first give your baby solid foods, start with pureed vegetables—and not necessarily the sweetest ones such as sweet potatoes, carrots and squash. Help them develop an appetite for vegetables of all kinds and not expect to exclusively eat sweet foods.

No special-order meals.
When your children graduate to eating regular foods, make just one meal for the whole family. Don't make mac and cheese for the kids when the adults are eating grilled chicken and kale salad. Make healthy foods everyone will enjoy.

Encourage them to try at least one bite of every food on their plate.
You don't want to engage in an epic battle, but do approach mealtime positively, with the expectation that your kids will at least try everything—and may very well clean their plates.

Don't use sweets as a reward.
This can actually sabotage the healthy eating habits you're trying to teach your children. Giving sweets, chips or soda as a reward can teach children to eat these foods to reward themselves when they're not hungry. Alternative rewards can include pencils, stickers, playing a favorite game or new art supplies.

Model healthy eating.
If they see you eating healthy foods, they'll want to eat them, too.

Cook together.
Even young children can do a little something to "help." Children are much more likely to eat something that they've helped to prepare.

Avoid labeling foods as "good" or "bad."
Instead, connect healthy foods to things your children care about or to goals they may have—such as being strong for swimming or doing well in school. Lean proteins help build muscles and brains. The vitamins, minerals and antioxidants in fruits and vegetables make your skin glow and your hair shiny.

Eat as a family at the table.
Life is busy, but research shows that if you can sit down and eat together at least three or four nights, children have better nutrition and are less likely to get in trouble at school.

Let kids have some say in what you serve.
Have kids taste the different foods on their plates and give them a grade—A, B, C, D or F. When they give high marks to healthy foods (especially vegetables!), serve them often.

ELEMENTARY SCHOOL

age 5–9 years

Helping Your Child Behave

Grade school is when discipline and self-control can take hold. Here's how to get to good.

Your 8-year-old has taken to refusing bedtime. After a few nights of patiently alternating between cajoling and threatening, you finally lose it totally and start yelling at the top of your lungs–just like the kind of parent you didn't want to be. But you tell yourself you had to reinforce that there are rules, and that your child must follow them. Honestly, what else could you do?

Actually, a lot, say child-behavior experts. Often when parents run up against bad behavior in their kids, from fighting with siblings to refusing to do homework, they fall back on the "might makes right" theory (or simply give in to their anger and frustration and explode). But once you understand some basic behavior-modification concepts–and how your child's brain reacts to interpersonal exchanges–you can reduce the stress of keeping your kid in line. Follow the rules on the next pages to restore peace to your household.

DEVELOPMENT MILESTONES

ABOUT AGES 5–6

* Moves independently, negotiates obstacles in her path * Can run, skip, climb, dance, throw and catch * Can use scissors; writes letters * Rides a tricycle, scooter, bicycle * Can draw recognizable people, houses, planes, and cars * Self-confident but also able to be social with others * Can control emotions * Inquisitive * Can play alone or with others

ABOUT AGES 7–9

* Enjoys a variety of activities, from running and jumping to sports like soccer, baseball and basketball * Independent; may be solitary for short periods of time * May be moody but becomes more self-reliant * Not always able to control energy so becomes tired and irritable * Reads independently; may enjoy writing stories * Can do basic math in head

1 Model Good Behavior

First off, let's talk about you, the parent. One of the most powerful ways to teach children how to behave well is to behave well yourself. That means showing that you can be frustrated with something (the vacuum is broken!) without getting angry, and you stay calm even in the face of your child's whining or rage.

One reason this works is because of something that happens in special brain cells called "mirror neurons." These specialized neurons are a fairly new discovery, and scientists are excited about the implications. It's like this: When you watch someone do something–smile, yawn, reach for a cup–your mirror neurons activate in the same way they would if you were doing the same action yourself. In the words of one scientist, "They collapse the distinction between seeing and doing." And when they activate, they forge new neural connections for the future, just as if you actually had physically performed the action.

So as your child watches you navigate the world, even from a very young age, what she observes fires up all kinds of neural connections; she is learning, and filing away information. "The main point is that modeling, which is teaching by example, affects your child's behavior far more than telling him what to do–and far more than punishing him, too," says Alan Kazdin, PhD, a research professor emeritus of psychology and child psychiatry at Yale University.

2 Favor Praise Over Punishment

When your child is flagrantly disrespecting or disobeying you, punishing her seems like the logical way to say: This behavior must stop. But in fact, says Kazdin, that goes at it backward. "Giving attention to undesired behaviors actually increases the undesired behaviors, while giving attention to good behaviors increases good behaviors," he explains. How could that be so? Why wouldn't a child remember the punishment and decide not to repeat the behavior later? A clue is in the word "attention."

Attention of any kind–positive or negative–is a powerful incentive, especially for children, who can often feel they're not getting enough of yours. So if whining about buying candy leads to Mom leaning down and explaining

First–Day Jitters

Lunch is packed; clothes are laid out; backpack is ready. Make the first day of school—and every day after that— great, with these simple strategies.

Have a laugh. If your child feels anxious, help him vent by giving him the giggles. Tell a joke, have a pillow fight, chase him around the house—just making him laugh can relieve stress before he walks out the door.

Take time to cuddle. Give your child some extra snuggle time in the morning or before bed so she feels secure. And when she gets home, pay full attention as she tells you about her day.

Make goodbyes special. Start a parting ritual that will help her feel secure—a secret handshake, a big hug, a special saying. Or give her something small to hold on to, like a token or picture she can pull out.

Be early for pickup. Nobody wants to be the last kid picked up from school. Do your best to get there a few minutes early—it'll make both of you feel happier and less stressed-out.

why you can't have it right now, that can be perceived by the child as a positive outcome. Mom's paying attention! This is why, when it comes to minor misbehaviors that aren't dangerous, research suggests that parents should learn to simply ignore the "acting out," a process called "extinction" (as in, eventually the child extinguishes the behavior because it isn't getting results). But you can't just go around ignoring all bad behavior; you have to also help your child learn what good behavior is—and the rewards it will bring her.

For example, Kazdin and his team at the Yale Parenting Center and Child Conduct Clinic found in several studies that when parents changed their responses to behaviors—say, ignoring screaming and whining but giving a lot of praise and attention when their child asked nicely for something—the child learned that asking nicely is the better, more reliable way to get attention. Giving frequent, effusive praise for behavior you want to encourage is key, says Kazdin. It's much more common for parents to call out misbehavior than to praise something done well. So flip the script: Rather than thinking about what you want your child not to do, figure out how you do want him to act. Then tell him exactly how you want him to behave. "When you get mad at your sister, I want you to use words or come tell me about it or just get away from her. No matter what, I want you to keep your hands to yourself."

Then, when he does something that's a step in the right direction, praise it specifically and lavishly. "You got mad at Sally, but you used words and didn't hit or kick, and that's great!" Add a smile or a touch, like a hug, kiss or pat on the shoulder, says Kazdin. "Verbal praise is more effective when it's augmented by another sense." Next, keep practicing; this technique requires repetition. When your child does even the smallest thing well, praise

Elementary school is an exciting time in your child's life, with each day a new learning adventure!

Fast Facts

* A child's brain reaches its full size at about age 5, but won't stop developing until he's in his mid-20s.
* From ages 3 to 8, a child's brain tissue uses twice the energy an adult brain uses.
* Students should spend about 10 times their grade level (in minutes) on homework per night. For first-graders, that's 10 minutes.

School Savvy

Kids advance in a variety of stages, some earlier than others. But here are some basics you can expect your first-grader to learn.

READING AND WRITING

First grade is when kids really become readers—they start learning strategies to figure out the meaning of unfamiliar words, read out loud and read for both pleasure and schoolwork. They'll also start making up detailed stories and writing them down.

SCIENCE

Kids are usually eager to jump into firsthand investigations of the world around them, whether it's watching a plant grow from a seed or monitoring an electric circuit.

MATH

By first grade, most kids can count up to at least 200 and count backward from 20. They know the difference between odd and even numbers, how to chart numbers on a number line and use more advanced strategies for addition and subtraction. They can count sides of shapes, read a map and follow other detailed directions.

it directly. Go beyond saying, "You're such a good boy!" and exclaim, "You did such a great job of cleaning up!" or, "Wow, you asked so nicely for that cookie–I'm proud of you!"

3 | Do Time-Outs and Time-Ins

One form of "punishment" that Kazdin feels can be effective is time-outs–but less because it's "punishing," and more because it simply withdraws all attention. It's like taking the oxygen away from a fire. The technique grew out of animal studies, in which researchers changed behavior in the animal by briefly removing reinforcers for the reward-earning behaviors (like getting food by pressing a lever). It can work very well in humans, says Kazdin, but only if you do it right.

The time-out should be brief and immediate–it has to be very clear why it's happening. And longer is not better, especially with younger children. "Only the first minute or so is essential for changing a child's behavior, and after 10 minutes even a well-deserved time-out becomes counterproductive," Kazdin says. Then, praise her compliance, which is a powerful reward.

Equally important to a time-out, though, is what Kazdin calls a time-in: what the parents are praising when the child isn't being punished. Time-in is when you really reinforce the behaviors you want to see, and it is more powerful than a time-out. So, for instance, if you've given a time-out for hitting, then you need to notice and reward the times when your child doesn't hit when she's frustrated. As always, the really important learning happens when your child is getting cues about what will earn him rewards–behaviors that, when he's able to control himself, will make you say, "Good job!"

Are You a Rage Ball or an Explainer?

These are the two most common responses to a child's misbehavior, says child psychologist Alan Kazdin, PhD—and you may have tried both at different times. The rage ball goes ballistic, ranting and screaming, while the explainer calmly and gently explains why the behavior is wrong. "But they're both probably ineffective in changing the behavior," says Kazdin. "That's because they fixate on the behavior, which reinforces it by giving it attention. Then they try to punish or to talk it into oblivion, both of which rarely work."

WHAT'S WRONG

The problem with the ballistic approach, says Kazdin, is that it doesn't teach what to do, and rarely even teaches what *not* to do. It can also have unintended consequences when your child models your own behavior by going ballistic with friends or at school. On the other hand, while explaining why—for instance, we should treat others nicely and not hit them— is a good message, it's not likely to change your child's behavior. Knowing that what you're doing is wrong does not necessarily trigger an end to the behavior, says Kazdin.

WHAT'S RIGHT Tell your child exactly what you want him to do, and when it's appropriate. "I want you to stay calm and not yell or raise your voice when I say no to you." "Don't confuse improving his behavior with improving his moral understanding," says Kazdin. Then, when he approximates this behavior next time, praise him warmly. There is a time to talk about how we should behave and treat others—but it's not in the midst of a meltdown.

TWEENS

age 10-12 years

Friends and Frenemies

The new word on boosting self-confidence: It grows through challenge and achievement, not quick praise and easy trophies.

C hildhood has always been emotionally rough-and-tumble, replete with cries of "He pushed me!" and "Emma said she doesn't like me anymore!" But in these days of worried helicopter parents hovering overhead, the social playing field seems more fraught than ever. "Our society has an obsession with groups and friends, and we're preoccupied with socializing children," says parent coach Meghan Leahy. "Kids are constantly receiving the message that you need to have many friends to show your social status." Leahy says she sees more cliques and groups forming at younger ages, and even bullying behaviors that in the past typically didn't start until late middle school or high school are cropping up as early as kindergarten.

That said, developmentally speaking, making a friend in school is every bit as important as getting an A. Learning how to form peer relationships is a critical skill that your child will use throughout his life–so, inevitably, he must enter the fray and learn how to get along. Your job is not to navigate that path with him, but rather to help him gain the skills he needs to find his own way. Here are some guidelines for doing exactly that.

Empathize Rather Than Instruct

Your daughter comes to you in tears because Sally said she doesn't want to play with her anymore. As parents, our first impulse is to try to fix it. In a word: Don't. "You can't solve your child's problem for her," says Amanda Mintzer, PsyD, a psychologist at the Child Mind Institute in New York City. "A lot of type-A personalities, myself included, want to jump in and solve it and make it better. But that might not even be what your child is asking for." What she does crave is your ear and your sympathy, so the first step is to acknowledge your child's feelings–whether it's hurt, confusion, frustration or anger. Let her talk through it in as much detail as she wants, and be an active listener, entering into and validating her feelings. It does hurt! It can be tough to see your child suffer, but she is learning how to work her own way through her emotions. Your job is to stay calm and lend an ear.

Don't Bring Your Own Anxieties Into It

This process is partly about learning to tolerate our own discomfort, says Mintzer. "When your child is upset, it's distressing for you, and you want to end the distress for both of you." That can lead you to offer bromides like, "It's OK, honey, you'll feel better tomorrow," but no matter how old you are, adds Mintzer, "nobody likes to be told what they're feeling." And in the midst of pain, it's hard for your child to believe that things will get better.

Parents should also beware of transferring too many of their own social expectations on children, says Mary Rooney, PhD, a psychologist who specializes in ADHD and disruptive behavior disorders. "Kids need just one or two good friends," Rooney says. "You don't have to worry about them being the most popular kid in their class."

Broaden the Perspective

After empathizing, you can lead the conversation to thinking about where her ex-friend Sally was coming from, says Mintzer.

DEVELOPMENT MILESTONES

* Increases coordination and strength
* Physically develops proportions that are less like a kid and more like an adult
* May begin puberty, with signs like sexual development, increased body odor and voice changes (for boys)
* Tends to develop a strong group identity and increasingly defines self through peers
* Intellectually, starts to move from solely concrete thinking (focusing on the here and now) to more abstract thinking (about issues not associated with a specific instance)

* Often feels strong emotions as hormonal changes start to occur (especially in girls)
* May experience swift and sudden mood shifts, i.e., be laughing one moment and crying the next, often for no rational reason
* Is becoming exposed to increasing peer pressure
* Is mentally ready to understand and be taught about the potential consequences of actions
* Changing bodies means that personal hygiene is gaining in importance (give as much support as possible to help them stay confident)

"You could suggest that maybe Sally is going through something you don't know about. We don't know why she said that, but it hurts, and it's not fair. You don't have to like it, but you might just have to accept it, for now." That in itself is a learning experience: You can't make everyone like you, and that's a lesson everyone needs to absorb.

Beyond that, though, these moments can be an opportunity to look objectively with your child at how he is perceived by others, and what he contributes to various social situations. For instance, you could ask your child about things that put him off from other kids–say, bragging, not being a good sport, taunting or teasing. And on the other

The Shy Child

Not everyone is a social butterfly—but every parent wants her child to be socially comfortable. That can be difficult for the 20 percent of children who are "born shy." Shyness is one of the most clearly identifiable heritable traits, says psychologist Gail Gross, PhD. "We can see it in brain scans," Gross says. "And you can see it in your child at only a few months of age. A shy baby is more sensitized to other people, and might put her head in your neck or seem anxious when confronted with new sounds, people or any kind of change. Shy children have a low threshold for the unexpected."

That said, biology is not destiny, Gross adds. Parents can affect how that genetic predisposition is expressed by making changes in their child's social environment. Rather than protecting your child from social experiences, Gross says, "start desensitizing her by exposing her, little by little, in a safe place, to what she fears." Begin by inviting other toddlers over for a short period of time—even just five or 10 minutes at first—and reassure your child that the visit will be brief. "By keeping your word, you are building your child's trust and security while creating a new, positive behavior. Eventually she will become calmer and more comfortable around other children."

7 WAYS TO FOSTER INDEPENDENCE

Let your tween decide:

1
Which after-school activities to join

2
Which family activities to do

3
Which friends to invite over

4
How to spend her allowance

5
What he wants to wear to school

6
What restaurant to go to for dinner

7
When to do her homework

side, ask him about the kids he does like to play with: What are they like? This can help give your child a perspective on himself and the children around him, and he can begin to ask himself: What kind of person do I want to be?

Help Your Child Build Social Muscles

Social skills are exactly that: skills, meaning something to be learned. When children are toddlers and just beginning to exercise those skills, parents can help by talking them through playdates before they happen.

Banish Bullying

It may seem like bullying is alarmingly on the rise, but according to reports by the U.S. Department of Health and Human Services, that's mainly because of increased awareness. Studies suggest that bullying may actually be declining. That said, a significant number of children encounter it. Three-quarters of young people say they have seen bullying in their schools. Most of this bullying is not physical, but verbal and social: name-calling, teasing, spreading rumors or lies, leaving people out. Despite the high profile of cyberbullying, in the form of email, blogging or social media, studies show it accounts for only about 10 percent of cases. Other research shows that many children don't tell parents or teachers about being bullied, but they also point out a solution: When bystanders intervene in a bullying incident, in 57 percent of cases, the behavior stops within 10 seconds. The takeaway is to keep the lines of communication open with your children, talking openly about bullying and encouraging them to get help when they see it happening or experience it themselves.

Children learn best from the natural consequences of their actions, explains Jamie Howard, PhD, a clinical psychologist at the Child Mind Institute, which is why it's so important to let them practice socializing in a warm, supportive setting. Then, when you review how it went later, focus on the good behavior you want to promote.

Of course, that's not going to work when your child is already older and has developed her own social circle. But some of the same lessons–such as being a good friend and staying positive, not gossiping or going negative–still hold true.

It can also help to be around your child's friends, albeit in a nonintrusive way. Allow her to invite a companion to your family movie or game night, or let her bring a pal along on a weekend adventure.

You may find that your child is naturally drawn to social experiences and eager to engage with others–or that he seems to prefer considerable time alone. The latter is not necessarily shyness, which involves anxiety, says Gail Gross, PhD, EdD, MEd. It may simply be that he is an introvert rather than an extrovert. "Shy" and "introverted" are actually different animals, says Gross. "An introvert is not distressed by other people, but simply needs time alone to contemplate and feel restored. Extroverts, on the other hand, are restored by being with other people and in a stimulating environment, and can feel down when they're alone." If your child seems comfortable with socializing but also prizes "quiet time" spent reading or drawing on her own, just make sure she gets enough of both.

Bottom line: "Real, deep and meaningful friendships take time," says Leahy. "Meanwhile, emphasize that your child is a valued and needed part of your family. You can promote her growth without laying on the pressure."

They're not little kids or teens. Give them the support they need for this peer-pressure-filled time.

131

Getting Her Period

Most girls begin menstruating between the ages of 10 and 15 (the average is age 12). Find ready answers to her biggest questions.

How long will it last?
Most cycles have two to three days of heavier bleeding, followed by two to four days of lighter flow.

Can I use a tampon?
There's no "right" age to start using a tampon. It can help to practice with slender tampons so you get used to the feeling of using them. Having trouble? Place a little petroleum jelly on the tip so it slides in more easily. Change a tampon every three to four hours.

How do I know when it will come next? Periods are notoriously irregular in the early days, so don't be surprised to go five or six weeks without it. Keep track of your cycles so you'll get a better idea of when it may come.

What can I do to reduce cramps? Medications like ibuprofen and naproxen can block the effects of cramp-causing hormones. You can also use a hot-water bottle, do some light exercise and try massaging your lower belly.

WHEN PUBERTY STRIKES

Boys and girls develop at different ages and stages, but in general, there are changes you can expect to see.

BODY CHANGES	AGE		BODY CHANGES
	GIRLS	BOYS	
Breasts begin to develop	7–13	10–13	Testicles enlarge; scrotum turns darker, coarser
Pubic hair begins to grow	8–14	10–15	Pubic hair begins to grow
Vagina grows longer, labia more pronounced	8–15	11–14½	Penis begins to grow longer and fuller
Body grows taller and heavier	9–14	10½–16	Body grows taller and heavier
Menstruation begins	9–16	11–17	Becomes capable of ejaculating semen
Hair begins to grow under arms	11–16	12–17	Hair begins to grow under arms
Glands in skin and scalp produce more oil	11–16	12–17	Glands in skin and scalp produce more oil

Source: American Academy of Pediatrics

Secrets of Self-Esteem

The new word on boosting self-confidence: It grows through challenge and achievement, not quick praise and easy trophies.

A few decades ago, "self-esteem" became a thing with our kids. Not that it hadn't existed before, but a school of thought arose that many problems for children stemmed from "low self-esteem." Thus began the era where kids are rewarded just for showing up—rather than for excelling—and parents offer routine encouragement ("Good job!"). There were some flaws in this plan, though: The research didn't really support it, and these interventions didn't increase self-esteem.

"High self-esteem is not an elixir to get you through life," says Alan Kazdin, PhD, a research professor emeritus of psychology and child psychiatry at Yale University. "I've dealt with aggressive and violent children who have higher self-esteem than average." Self-esteem, Kazdin feels, comes from feeling competent—playing an instrument or sticking with a tough school project.

The first step is encouraging your child to explore many areas so she can find things that spark her passion. But there are other ways to help your child grow that proud part of herself. Here, some steps to take:

* Praise specifically.
Saying, "You're so smart!" or (worse) "You're so pretty!" is counterproductive, says Laura Markham, PhD, founding editor of ahaparenting.com. Such compliments are not objective or provable, and your child may not believe them. Be specific and praise effort at least as much as outcome: "You're working so hard on that homework" or "You cleaned up with only one reminder. Thank you!" That helps them see themselves as having autonomy and self-control.

* Let them overhear praise.
Perhaps even more powerful than direct praise is allowing your child to hear you extolling them to someone else, says Markham. When he catches you saying on the phone, "He was so helpful today" or "He and his sister are really working things out," he's more likely to believe that you really mean it.

* Help them fight self-labeling.
Children do this often when they feel they have failed: Rather than thinking, "I didn't do very well on that spelling test," it's "I'm so stupid!" You can help your child reject negative self-talk by offering objective facts—not acing one test doesn't mean someone is stupid—and reframing setbacks as temporary, and part of a progression. "Your 'power word' here is 'yet,'" says Markham. As in, "You just haven't learned to spell that word yet." Then help your child move forward by discussing steps that will improve her work in the future, so she looks at it more through a problem-solving lens. "It's only one test. What can we do so you know the words before the next test?" This support teaches her that her actions will have a big impact on her future success.

* Challenge stereotypes.
As they approach puberty, kids get messages about what makes them a successful girl or boy. Girls see images of female "perfection" in media, pushing the idea that looks are of premium value. Boys are pressured to be "tough" and self-sufficient in order to be a "man." Try to experience media together so you can call out stereotypes, says Rachel Busman, PsyD, a psychologist at the Child Mind Institute. You could praise a boy on TV for showing empathy or vulnerability and point out women honored for achievement rather than for how they look.

TEENS

age 13-18 years

Risk and Reward

Your teen's brain is expanding by leaps and bounds, and veering between impulse and self-control.

News flash: Teens are impulsive and prone to risk-taking behaviors. This is, of course, not news to any parent of an adolescent–or anyone who recalls their own teenage years. It's such a trope that it has been immortalized in countless movies over the years: wild parties when parents are away (*Risky Business*), messing up a parent's car (*Ferris Bueller's Day Off*, *Sixteen Candles*), and bad decisions to go into dark woods at night (every teen slasher film ever made).

Recent brain science has begun to explain this near-universal aspect of adolescence, and it boils down to a mismatch in brain development. The "executive function" prefrontal cortex, which deals with decision-making, planning and self-control, matures

DEVELOPMENT MILESTONES

✱ Boys start to hit their growth spurts while girls start to slow down. By the end of high school, most girls will have reached their full height; boys are often still growing ✱ Tends to be frequently hungry (especially boys—see growth spurt, above). Boys ages 14 to 18 typically need between 2,200 and 3,200 calories a day, according to the Academy of Nutrition and Dietetics—as many as 4,000, if very active ✱ Typically shows an increased ability to reason, make educated guesses and separate fact from fiction; starts to reason more abstractly and is able to think about ways to deal with hypothetical situations ✱ Don't worry, it's not you: When 14 or 15 years old, children are often "embarrassed" by their parents and driven to be accepted by their peers; but between the ages of 16 and 18, they usually come around and are more eager to communicate with their parents.

actions, says Wang, whether it's unprotected sex, driving after drinking, or using illegal drugs. The chemistry that encourages such behavior can be seen in fMRI scans, where teenagers' brains show more activity than adults' do in the ventral striatum–a region that signals anticipation of a reward–while playing a game of chance and risk. The rewards for risk-taking are hardwired into teens' brains, and egged on by the release of the "pleasure transmitter" dopamine, which goes up at puberty. Dopamine can also drive what's called "novelty-seeking" behavior: Anything new and different can seem attractive to teens, especially when they're with other teens.

All that said, experts say there is still plenty that parents can do to help guide and protect their children through puberty and adolescence. Much of it involves setting up family structures and ways of communicating early on, so that you don't suddenly morph into the "bad cop" mom when your child hits age 12. One thing to keep in mind is that the (more risk-taking) social-emotional system is not always "active," says Alan Kazdin, PhD, a research professor emeritus of psychology and child psychiatry at Yale University. One well-known activator is the presence of peers–even if they're not directly encouraging certain behaviors–as well as generally being emotionally excited or stimulated (which is often synonymous with being with peers, Kazdin adds).

Postponing and limiting contact with peers who engage in risky behavior and replacing that contact with other activities can help, he says. "Sometimes even out-and-out distraction and pandering–'Let's go clothes shopping again!'–isn't the worst strategy," says Kazdin. "Some parents feel they're playing for time, telling themselves, 'If I can just get my kid through adolescence in one piece, everything will be OK,' but there's some wisdom in that." You can also try these

about two years later than the subcortical areas that participate in emotion and reward. That makes adolescence a unique time, says Sam Wang, PhD, associate professor of neuroscience at Princeton University, in which "the balance between impulse and restraint may be quite different than either childhood or adulthood."

Numerous studies show that teenagers tend to underestimate the consequences of their research-supported approaches to keeping things relatively calm and safe during the whirlwind of your child's adolescence. "There's not a magic bullet or a pill to contain teen risk, and some of these ideas may seem mundane, but they're important over the long haul," says Kazdin.

Monitor Your Child

That means keeping track of where he is, what he's doing and who he's with.

Teenagers with parents who do this routinely have been shown to be much less likely to engage in sexual activity or illicit drug use. "If you feel awkward or uncool about hounding your poor child, remember that there's a strong dose-response relation between monitoring and decreased risk," says Kazdin. That means more intense monitoring is associated with greater reduction in risky behavior. But it's not simply cop-like surveillance, he adds.

Sleep Tight

You may be yawning, but your teen's not even tired. He still needs about eight to 10 hours of sleep a night, however. Help him get it.

During the teenage years, biological sleep patterns shift toward later doze-off and wake times—so it's natural to not be able to fall asleep before 11 p.m., according to the National Sleep Foundation (NSF). Sleep is also when the body's pituitary gland produces essential growth hormones. You probably can't change your teens' alarm clock on school days, but you can help him get more Z's with these strategies from the NSF.

* Avoid late-night stimulation. Have your teen turn off her devices at least an hour before bed (exposure to the light emitted from smartphones and computers can interfere with natural sleep cycles) and avoid eating, drinking or exercising too close to bedtime.

* Make sleep a priority. Keep a diary and see what you need to change to get him to bed on time.

* Factor in naps. If her schedule permits, naps are a way to offer a quick pick-me-up. Just avoid napping too close to bedtime or for too long (more than 20 minutes).

* Turn her room into a sleep haven. Keep it cool, dark and quiet—install blackout shades, if necessary. When morning comes, open up the shades and let natural light act as a wake-up call. Keep electronics out of the bedroom entirely—charge devices in another room.

* Be consistent. Try to establish firm bed and wake times, even on weekends. Having a consistent sleep schedule helps your teen feel less tired and allows the body to sync with its natural patterns.

Your teenage boy has 50% more testosterone now than he had before he reached adolescence.

Instead, it also involves creating a warm and close-knit family where monitoring is normal and, importantly, mutual. "You can model that by talking to your child about your day, at the dinner table or in the car, and begin early, so it's a natural part of your family structure." Another form of low-key monitoring that indulges your child's craving for time with peers is to make your home a place where she can bring friends while you're there.

Your Teen's Brain

While they are nearly full-size by age 6, our brains are still maturing well into our mid-20s. That's especially true of the prefrontal cortex, the area of the brain responsible for reasoning, controlling impulses and decision making. Other brain changes during adolescence include a rapid increase in the connections between brain cells, helping to make brain pathways more effective.

Because of these changes, teens are more likely to act on impulse and misread social cues. They're also more likely to get into accidents or fights, and engage in risky behavior.

Build Bonds and Model Behavior

Set up a structure of values at home, beginning in elementary school, which embraces schoolwork, time with family and extracurricular activities. "Building these habits early in life has been shown to decrease later risk-taking," says Kazdin. To strengthen family bonds that will become especially crucial in the teen years, establish routines and rituals that tie you together: making special holidays and meals, doing your weekly errands together, even having family "inside jokes." It's also important to model the behavior you expect from your kids, like valuing hard work and not giving in to frustration or discouragement when it inevitably occurs. It also involves not avoiding talking explicitly about drug use and the attendant dangers. "Research shows that parents who talk about the riskiness of substance abuse, and who don't engage in it themselves, measurably decrease their children's risk," says Kazdin.

Help Them to Become Competent

When your child finds something she's "good at," it has a powerful protective effect during the teen years—and is also essential to her overall self-esteem. Whether it's music, sports or working with animals at a shelter, building competence in something she can continue to engage in through adolescence has been shown to be protective. It's especially helpful when peers are involved in structured activities, like practices and games, or rehearsals and concerts, where adults are also part of the picture.

Your teen's brain isn't mature enough to make good decisions, so make sure you're around to provide good advice.

Build Strong Bones

Adolescence is a key period for building a strong skeleton. Make sure your teen is getting the calcium he or she needs to develop bone mass.

From ages 11 to 15, bones are developing quickly; nearly half of all bone is formed during this time. By age 17, kids have established more than 75 percent of their adult bone mass. The more they put into their bone bank now, the stronger their skeletons will be. Make sure they get enough calcium in their diet to build strong bones for life. Nutrition guidelines recommend that children ages 9 to 18 get 1,300 mg of calcium daily. See chart (below) for healthy options.

Food Source	Calcium (mg)
8 oz. low-fat or skim milk	300
½ cup cottage cheese	300
1 cup yogurt	450
1 oz. mozzarella cheese	200
1 cup broccoli	180
1 cup spinach	240
1 cup cooked garbanzo beans	80
8 oz. calcium-fortified orange juice	300
4 oz. calcium-fortified tofu	250–750
½ to 1 cup calcium-fortified cereals	250–1,000
1 slice calcium-fortified bread	150–200
1 packet instant oatmeal	150
1 oz. almonds	80

Source: USDA Database

Be Close and Connected

When a child feels close to a parent–loved, wanted and listened to–he is at much lower risk of engaging in dangerous behaviors, says Kazdin. Researchers have found a middle ground in parental control that's the most effective: neither too loose (permissive and uninvolved) nor too tight (authoritarian and controlling). The latter especially can be counterproductive, as teens who are trying out their wings can be triggered to be even *more* challenging if they're in an environment that feels to them like it's unnecessarily rigid. Finding that middle ground means having explicitly expressed household rules and boundaries, but also listening with an open mind to your child's point of view and "making as few decisions as possible based simply on 'Because I said so,'" says Kazdin. "Compromise when you can, and let some things go when you can," he adds. "Consider giving a little when it comes to things like bedtime, curfew or a messy room. That actually helps you gain credibility and control when the topic shifts to more substantial issues." After all, spending a late night watching movies is far safer than being out till 4 a.m. with friends. Lastly, says Kazdin, don't give in to the "slippery-slope logic" that if you let one thing go, your child will go wild. "That's typically the opposite of what happens. If you go to war over every minor thing, you lose both the minor and the major. And it pits you against your child." There's a metaphor that Kazdin prefers to the "battle and war" idea, and it's the image of sailing. Picture sailing a ship toward the goal of a well-adjusted, functional adulthood for your child. "This requires tacking, which can look like you're veering away from the goal," says Kazdin. "But tacking is often the best path to the goal in the end." And while it may feel like you're sometimes going through a hurricane, you will reach the shore together.

How to Talk Substances

Don't be an ostrich! The Child Mind Institute advocates having a sit-down discussion with your teen about substance abuse. Their advice:

☐ **Spell out rules.** Research shows that kids tend to be safer when parents set limits—even if they don't always follow them. Rules also help your teen to say no and use parents as an excuse.

☐ **Explain your reasons.** Be honest and rational; for instance, heroin is riskier than marijuana. But the consequences for drug use and underage drinking are real: getting cut from a team, having unwanted sexual encounters, and driving drunk.

☐ **Let them speak.** Give your child a chance to express feelings—and speak to her like the adult you want her to become. Encourage a dialogue so she'll be honest with you in the future.

☐ **Consider amnesty.** If you have an "amnesty policy," your teen can call for help without getting into trouble, as opposed to hiding his behavior and being in an even riskier situation. For example, if he (or his designated driver) is drunk, he can call you for a ride or cab fare instead of putting himself at risk. He can go to bed without punishment, and you can have a sober talk about drinking in the morning.

Don't be surprised if your teen tests his boundaries—but don't close yourself off to communication, either.

CHAPTER 4

Navigating the World at Large

At some point, your kids will make their own way.
Here's how to make sure they thrive no matter what path they take.

How to Raise a Money– Smart Kid

Finances may seem like a grown-up topic, but it's
not too early to start teaching your child the value of a buck.

You might think your children are too young to think about finances, but chances are, they're old enough to handle it–and you're not discussing it enough. One of the biggest mistakes parents can make when it comes to raising money-savvy kids is to not bring it up at all.

"As a parent, you have to realize that you're training your child to become a great adult," says Rachel Cruze, co-author of *Smart Money Smart Kids*. "In order to be successful, they have to know how to handle money, and the best place for them to learn that is from the home. Don't be afraid or intimidated by it." Here's how to get the conversation started.

Our Cashless Society

When most of us were growing up, bills arrived in the mail and were paid by mailing back with a check. Your parents may have gone to a bank and deposited their paychecks.

Credit cards weren't widely accepted, or maybe they were used just for emergencies. We watched cash changing hands daily.

Today, many of us use little to no cash most of the time. "Many parents now do everything with credit or debit cards, and pay bills online. Kids sometimes don't even get to see money," says Cruze.

That's too bad, because the fewer opportunities your children have to see how money is both received and given, the harder it is for them to appreciate its value. "Cash transactions create teachable moments," says Cruze. For example: You head to the supermarket to buy your weekly groceries, pay in cash and maybe even get some change–all of which your child sees at the checkout. Now think about when you simply swipe your credit card. Whether it's for two items or 20, it all looks the same. So it's difficult for your child to understand how much money you are spending.

Then there's the fact that paying virtually rather than physically can also do harm to your family's budget. A paper published in the *Journal of Experimental Psychology: Applied* found that people tend to overspend when using a credit card versus cash. "It's more difficult to part with money when you're physically counting out the bills. And that helps you make better, more careful decisions," notes Beth Kobliner, author of *Making Your Kid a Money Genius (Even if You're Not).*

Still not ready to give up your Apple Pay? That doesn't mean you can't turn the moment into a money lesson. If they're old enough, explain to your kids what's happening when you swipe your credit card or pay with your phone, suggests Cruze. "Let them know, 'This isn't just magic money,'" Cruze says. "Make sure they see the bank in person and tell them, 'There's a bank that we pass on the way home. That's where our money is.' Have conversations and be much more intentional about it."

The cash lesson is especially important when it's your kids who are getting the money. "I really encourage parents to make an effort to use cash with kids–especially if they are giving them an allowance," says Kobliner. "There are apps out there that will let you pay an allowance to your kid in digital tokens or 'beans.' But giving your kids cash is the simplest and smartest way to go. It's tangible and real in a way that you don't get with any other form of money."

Start Young

We should start talking to our kids about money as soon as possible, says Kobliner. Kids are able to grasp basic money concepts like value and exchange by age 3.

"This sounds very young to a lot of people, but a 3-year-old understands the cause and effect of working and getting paid," adds Cruze. "By this age, kids might ask questions about money. Don't shy away from that as a parent. Dig into the conversation when your kids bring up the topic of money."

Encourage your child to split her money into saving, spending and donating to worthy causes.

In fact, good money habits start early. "Research has shown that many good habits associated with money-management skills are really solidified by age 7," notes Kobliner. Of course, if your kids are already past that age, don't stress out–there are plenty of learning opportunities for older kids, too. "Take advantage of everyday teachable moments, like going to the grocery store with your fourth-grader or encouraging your middle-schooler to save some of her babysitting money," says Kobliner. Other teachable money moments could be showing your child how you check the receipt after purchasing something before you leave the store, just to make sure you weren't charged incorrectly for something. Or you could explain to your child why you prioritize certain items over others when you shop. You might explain why you bought the yogurt that's on sale, but then splurged for an item like organic chicken.

Put It Into Practice

Keep looking for ways to teach your kids about handling money in daily transactions. "If you're going shopping with your kid and she wants something that you know is going to blow your budget, use it as an opportunity to talk about financial trade-offs. Explain that she could buy the trendy shoes everyone wants or get two T-shirts, a pair of jeans and less-trendy shoes for the same amount," says Kobliner.

And keep up the dialogue. "Kids understand more information than their parents give them credit for," notes Cruze. "And if you're not the one talking and teaching them about money, who will be? The car dealer they meet when they're 25 years old and trying to buy a brand-new car? Or the bank? Or the credit card company? If it's under your control, you have an advantage as the parent to really lift them up and help them understand the best choices they can make."

Should I Give an Allowance?

When it's safe for them to handle it, allow preschoolers to use coins or paper money to play 'store' or 'bank' at home. You can also ask your child to help you pick out items at the real grocery store. Even kids as young as 3 years old might be ready for an allowance to help gain an understanding of the value of money. That amount can grow as they do (experts generally recommend a dollar per year of age). But try not to link an allowance to chores. "Chores should be tasks that kids do because they are motivated to help, not because their allowance depends on it. Because: What happens when they decide it's not worth that dollar to do it?" asks author Beth Kobliner.

If you want to pay extra for tasks around the house, consider doing so for "special" jobs, like cleaning out the garage. "But there's really no right or wrong way to do an allowance. If you find a system that works, keep doing it."

When Hard Times Hit

Hiding financial trouble—like losing your job—from kids generally isn't a good idea. "Be truthful but age-appropriate about money troubles when talking to your kids. Even if you have to cut back on spending, emphasize that you will get through this together as a family—and avoid language that is going to cause them worry or stress," advises author Beth Kobliner.

If your budget is tight, tell younger children that you're going to be cooking at home as a family more, rather than going out to eat. You can show your children how you browse for online coupons and deals when buying something online to save money. If your finances mean you have to cut out things like a big family vacation, give your children a heads-up and let them know that you'll still be doing fun, free activities around town. You can share more information about your financial situation with older children when it's appropriate—especially when you're talking about planning for college, Kobliner adds.

4 MONEY MISTAKES TO STOP MAKING

You're probably guilty of a few of these bad money habits.

1 **You fight in front of your kids.**
A study of college kids found that those who had seen their parents argue about money were more likely to misuse credit cards. Keep your arguments behind closed doors.

2 **You cosign on a credit card.**
Your kid should sign up for a credit card only if and when she has enough money to pay it off herself, advises Beth Kobliner.

3 **You hide your mistakes.**
"Humanize the topic," suggests Rachel Cruze. "You might share, '[I] took out a credit card in college and racked up all these bills, and I regret it to this day.'"

4 **You've become a human ATM.**
Plenty of kids tell their parents, "I need $10," and all too often, the parent's reaction is, "Sure, here you go," says Cruze. "They should know that eventually they'll need to work for it. Teach them you have to go to work in order to make money to survive. Understanding that money comes from work—and not just you—is a huge foundation point for them."

Money Smarts at Every Age

TODDLERS AND PRESCHOOLERS

Teach toddlers by giving them a few coins for doing extra chores, like helping you put the groceries away (but not for their regular chores). "Tell them, 'You just were a big help.' Then pay them instantly with physical money to understand the concept of working and getting paid," says author Rachel Cruze.

When they're 5, you can start more-structured money lessons. "I tell people to use three envelopes and label them: giving, saving and spending. Now, when the child gets paid, he can divide the money into those categories and start saving up for something he wants," says Cruze.

This helps your child learn to be patient, she adds. "Developing a sense of delayed gratification is bedrock when it comes to key money skills like saving and working for a living. Talk about things you wait for: a turn at the swings, your birthday. Explain that we also need to wait to buy things."

ELEMENTARY SCHOOLERS

"Now is a good time to talk about the importance of saving and why a bank is the safest place for your money," notes Beth Kobliner. If you haven't already, open a savings account at your neighborhood bank (a real brick-and-mortar one, not the virtual version). A savings account can help teach your child about interest, fees and other important financial concepts. Look for a bank that limits fees and pays relatively higher interest rates (similar to a version you would expect to open for yourself).

If your kid is starting to spend a lot of time online, or shops virtually, consider warning him or her about cybertheft. "This is a good time to stress how dangerous it can be to share personal information with strangers," advises Kobliner.

MIDDLE SCHOOLERS

Get your preteen children involved with saving up for something special. "You can offer to match their savings if they want something a little more expensive," suggests Cruze. For example: If a game costs $40, have them save $20 and then offer the rest as a reward for their hard work. "The older they are and the more they do, the more you can pay them."

Don't forget to emphasize the concept of saving for the future. Teach them to save $0.25 of every dollar they earn or receive, advises Cruze. You can even turn this into a financial lesson: "Talk about how compound interest works in an investment account." And middle schoolers should learn that a credit card is a loan that you have to pay off—not magic, invisible money.

HIGH SCHOOLERS

Sit your teen down and discuss the family's financial plan for college. "This stage is all about stressing why going to college is an important financial choice," says Kobliner. Research shows you'll earn $1 million more over your lifetime if you finish college than if you don't.

You should have a pretty good gauge of where you're at financially by the time your child is a freshman—and where you'll be in four years, says Cruze. "Let them know if you've started a college fund. Be honest with your kids about how much, if any, you can help with college. Tell them that it's their job to get good grades and find scholarships. Let them know if their expensive, out-of-state school or private 'dream college' may not be a reality. Help them make a choice that's smart for the family and for their future," she adds. This will help them make better decisions to emotionally and financially prepare for what's ahead.

X

30%: The percent
of young people
who admit to
bullying others

The Bullying Problem

One in four kids says they've been harassed in school, online
or with their peers, but parents often feel powerless to help.
Follow these tips for helping your child take control.

 few weeks ago, a Facebook friend reposted a message that her 12-year-old daughter had received on social media. "UR SO ANNOYING AND LEGIT NO ONE LIKES YOU. JUST KYS [Kill Yourself]." "I'm posting this as a public service message," my friend explained. "I'm not looking for comments or OMGs. Please talk to your children and tell them it's never OK to tell someone to kill themself.

Or that they are annoying, fat or ugly over and over. Words hurt."

Bullying today doesn't look the same as a generation ago, when sharp words exchanged in the hallways may have stung, but usually didn't go further than the schoolyard. Thanks to social media, the whole world can now be a playground for bullies to pick battles.

"Bullying has always been a problem," notes Nicole Beurkens, PhD, a licensed

psychologist based in Grand Rapids, Michigan. "But with the emergence of the internet and social media, it's reached a whole new realm."

The anonymity of social media means bullies can simply hide behind a device and spew their hatred to the entire planet. "It used to be the guy in the schoolyard picking on some little kid–now the idea of bullying goes far beyond that. The definition of what we think of as bullying has gotten much bigger," notes Betsy Brown Braun, a child-development and behavior specialist in Los Angeles.

While parents can often feel powerless when they see their child being victimized, you don't have to be helpless. Experts say that parents can actually play a key role in helping build children's confidence and reduce their exposure to bullies at any age.

Be Aware

Often words do the biggest damage, whether said to your child's face or online. Watch for signs that your child may be dealing with a bully: These include refusing to go to school; physical complaints, like frequent headaches or stomach pain; moodiness; difficulty sleeping; changes in eating habits; a sudden change in school performance; or avoiding peers.

Don't Go on the Attack

"Parents will try to immediately jump in and rescue their child from any potential harm being done," says Beurkens. But take time to listen to your child and help her talk about her feelings. "Involve your child in the process of how to handle the situation." This not only helps her develop coping skills, but also can help boost her self-esteem and confidence.

That said, there are clearly moments when it is appropriate for parents to step in and take control, notes Beurkens. "Any time there is a safety issue, or if things are not improving

✕

28% of U.S. students in grades 6 through 12 have experienced bullying.

Watch for signs of bullying, including refusing to go to school, physical complaints or a sudden change in academic performance or peer activity.

Get Help

These groups were established to help counter bullying in schools, online and wherever else kids interact.

* **Stopbullying.gov** offers up information from different government agencies on how to prevent and respond to bullying. (800-283-TALK)

* **PACER National Bullying Prevention Center (pacer.org/bullying)** provides information and resources for parents, students and educators to help prevent bullying as a social issue. (888-248-0822)

* **The Trevor Project** was created to support lesbian, gay, bisexual, transgender and queer young people ages 13 to 24 through times of crisis, including bullying. The Trevor Lifeline is for those who need a safe, judgment-free place to talk. (866-488-7386; thetrevorproject.org)

* **STOMP Out Bullying** was created to reduce and prevent bullying and digital abuse while deterring violence in schools, online and in communities nationwide through peer-mentoring programs in schools, social media campaigns and providing a live chat line for youth ages 13 to 24. (stompoutbullying.org)

or even getting worse, parents should get more directly involved," she says. If the incidents are taking place at school, talk to a school administrator; if you know the bully's parents, it can also help to talk to them directly, she adds.

Build Up His Self-Confidence

All bullies need victims, and most of them tend to look for someone who is vulnerable and seems to easily show fear. Help your child avoid developing a victim mentality by giving him a variety of tools that can help him feel more confident, says Brown Braun. "From a young age, teach your child to express his feelings and speak up for himself. It's important to be assertive and not tolerate bad behavior on the part of others."

Teach How Not to Respond

Bullies thrive on getting a reaction. Explain to your child that even if her feelings are being hurt, it's best not to let her guard down. Walking away is the best response she can give.

Raise Empathy

Most bullies start their behavior out of a problem with their own self-confidence, says Brown Braun. "I have told children as young as 4 that when someone is being mean to them, it's usually because he doesn't feel good about himself," she says. Explain to your child that some people may say or do mean things, but that it's not a reflection on the person being targeted.

Help Others When Necessary

Bullies often thrive on the response they get from others, so the more widespread the attacks, the better. So even if your child isn't the one being targeted, encourage her to step forward and say something. "It's not OK to tolerate bad behavior from anyone," says Brown Braun. Schools often encourage students to show kindness by standing up for kids who are being bullied–and parents should reinforce this message at home. It works: Research shows that when kids step in to stop an incident of bullying, more than half the time, the bully will back off within 10 seconds.

Not every kid may have the confidence to take that risk, and kids often feel powerless to help. But even deflecting attention off the bully with verbal interventions can make a difference. Ask whether someone knows when the science test will be or how the baseball playoffs are going. If that doesn't work, encourage your child to walk over and stand next to the person being targeted. Just being next to someone in a vulnerable situation can be enough to encourage the bully to get off the attack.

Show Kindness

Teach your child kindness and compassion by making sure you treat others as you want to be treated yourself. If someone cuts you off on the road or treats you unkindly, use this as an opportunity to model good behavior. Responding by speaking to someone in a mean or abusive tone can teach your child that it's OK to put other people down or be unkind.

What If Your Child Is the Bully?

Most of us don't like to think our child is capable of showing cruelty or being unkind, but the fact remains that kids still perpetrate bad behavior, even if that surprises their parents. "Bullying doesn't happen for no reason—it's not an accident. It's often a sign that a child's own needs aren't being met," says child development expert Betsy Brown Braun.

Bullying can start to surface as young as kindergarten, she notes, and can be a way of a child acting out to issues that may be happening in the home. "Often it's a matter that the child feels inadequate, and needs to create a response to those feelings."

And while it's easy to feel guilty, it's also important to address any underlying causes that may be taking place. Spend more time with your kids and listen to what they have to say. Acknowledge that there may be a problem, and see what you can do to help your child regain his or her own confidence. If that doesn't work, it may be time to seek help from a teacher, therapist or mental-health professional.

From Sadness to Suicide

Youth depression and suicide rates are on the rise,
but you can take action to keep your kids safe.

"I wish I was dead."

Today, when your child says these words, they cannot be brushed off as simple teen angst. There is a chance she is seriously considering taking her life.

The prevalence of 12- to 17-year-olds' reporting a major depressive episode within the past year increased by 37 percent between 2005 and 2014, according to a study published in *Pediatrics* in 2016. A major depressive episode includes symptoms such as depressed mood, sleep difficulties and loss of interest in pleasurable activities, lasting for at least two weeks.

About 5 percent of children and teens have depression at some point in their youth, according to the American Academy of Child and Adolescent Psychiatry. And the National Institute of Mental Health estimates that 3.1 million adolescents between 12 and 17 years old had at least one major depressive episode in 2016.

At the same time, rates of childhood and youth suicide and suicide attempts have also risen. The number of emergency-room visits for nonfatal self-inflicted injury increased 5.7 percent each year between 2008 and 2015, researchers reported in the *Journal of the American Medical Association*. Even more

Rates of childhood suicide and suicide attempts have risen dramatically in the past decade, making suicide a leading cause of death for kids.

alarming, the rate increased 18.8 percent annually for young women ages 10 to 14.

Suicide among teens and young adults has nearly tripled since the 1940s, according to the Centers for Disease Control and Prevention, with about 4,600 adolescents taking their own lives each year. While suicide was the 10th-leading cause of death for all ages in 2013, it's the third-leading cause of death for children ages 10 to 14–and the second-leading cause of death for people ages 15 to 34.

What's Happening?

Researchers are working to determine why this trend is happening, but experts say there is no single cause.

"Suicide, specifically youth suicide, tends to be complicated. It's very unhelpful to simplify it to one cause," says John Ackerman, PhD, suicide prevention coordinator of the Center for Suicide Prevention and Research at Nationwide Children's Hospital in Columbus, Ohio. "It worries me when

✕

Life can be a relentless hamster wheel of activity for your kid, and some can start to feel there's no escape from the pressure.

Don't wait until there is a crisis to bring up the topic of suicide—just talking about it won't put the idea in your child's head.

Don't Go It Alone

Get the information and support you need to support your kid. For more on childhood depression and suicide, consider these resources.

* **National Suicide Prevention Hotline** 1-800-273-8255

* **American Foundation for Suicide Prevention** afsp.org

* **Suicide Prevention Resource Center** sprc.org

* **American Academy of Child and Adolescent Psychiatry** aacap.org

* **American Association of Suicidology** suicidology.org

* **Effective Child Therapy** effectivechildtherapy.org

* **Info About Kids** infoaboutkids.org

media suggest it boils down to social media or bullying. That isn't a fair and accurate representation of youth suicide."

That isn't to say these aren't factors. In a 2017 study, San Diego State University and Florida State University researchers analyzed two nationally representative surveys of more than 500,000 teens in grades 8 through 12. They found that adolescents using social media daily were 13 percent more likely to report high levels of depressive symptoms than those using social media less often. And those spending at least three hours daily on electronic devices were 34 percent more likely to have at least one suicide-related outcome than those on the devices two or fewer hours a day.

But this study was correlational—and controversial. "Do I see the impact of technology and social media? Yes," Ackerman says. In addition to the loss of face-to-face contact and reduced sense of connection, too much time on social media can also lead to poor sleep and less physical activity, all of which can contribute to depression. But that doesn't mean social media is the sole cause of suicide-related behaviors.

Kids today also face a lot of demands. "When I see kids with depression or who contemplate suicide, they often feel there is no way out, no reprieve. Life is a hamster wheel of demands and tasks," says clinical psychologist Joe Dilley, PhD, author of *The Game Is Playing Your Kid: How to Unplug and Reconnect in the Digital Age*. When every day is school, then tutoring, practice, homework and bed, "they begin to feel, 'There's no way out of it, and I don't know if I can do it.'"

Speak Up

The best thing you can do to help reduce the risk of depression and suicide is to talk to your child, even if you haven't noticed any changes.

"Check in with your kids, whether or not they're showing warning signs," says Ackerman. You can frame the conversation about whether they have concerns about their friends. Ask: Do you or your friends ever feel like you are in a tremendous amount of pain? Have you ever thought about ending your life? Has suicide ever come up?

"It's uncomfortable, but do it repeatedly until it's not," Ackerman says. "It's so foreign to want to think about your child being in such pain that dying is more appealing than living, but it's important to have an honest, open discussion."

If your child isn't suicidal or depressed, having this talk will not put thoughts of suicide in their heads. And if he is, it's important to catch it as soon as possible. Continue open dialogues. "We want to take a catcher's-mitt approach," Dilley says. "We are receiving and fielding anything they're throwing out there, in a nonjudgmental way. This lets them know they can trust and confide in us."

And if they only say they're "fine," help them put words to their experiences. Rather than asking "What's the matter?" say, "Today must have sucked because you were up so late studying, and I know this teacher won't give you your grade until Friday."

If your child is contemplating suicide, opening up that conversation "can be an amazing relief for them," Ackerman says. "It's an opportunity to unburden themselves of the idea that life isn't worth living." Don't discount what they are saying. Listen and tell them you will get them the help they need. Take him to the ER immediately or call the National Suicide Prevention Lifeline.

"Don't wait until there is a crisis to bring this topic up," Ackerman says. "Preventing suicide is not one specific intervention, but rather a safety net involving many people."

Know the Signs

There is no one symptom of depression or suicidal thoughts. If one or more of these persists, seek help from a professional.

SIGNS OF DEPRESSION

✳ Frequent sadness, tearfulness, crying ✳ Decreased interest in activities or inability to enjoy previously favorite activities ✳ Hopelessness ✳ Persistent boredom, low energy ✳ Social isolation, poor communication ✳ Low self-esteem, guilt ✳ Extreme sensitivity to rejection or failure ✳ Increased irritability, anger or hostility ✳ Difficulty with relationships ✳ Frequent complaints of physical illnesses, such as headaches and stomachaches ✳ Frequent absences from school or poor performance in school ✳ Poor concentration ✳ A major change in eating and/or sleeping patterns ✳ Talk of, or efforts to, run away from home ✳ Thoughts or expressions of suicide or self-destructive behavior

SIGNS OF SUICIDAL THOUGHTS

✳ Thinking or talking about or threatening suicide ✳ Seeking a way to kill oneself ✳ Increased substance abuse (alcohol or drugs) ✳ Feelings of purposelessness, anxiety, being trapped or hopelessness ✳ Withdrawing from people and activities ✳ Expressing unusual anger, recklessness or mood changes ✳ Anxiety, agitation, inability to sleep, or sleeping a lot ✳ Engaging in risky activities ✳ Dramatic mood changes

Establish limits on use:
No more than
30–60 minutes a day for
kids under 10; 90 minutes
max for tweens;
and frequent breaks
for teens.

A Parent's Guide to Tech

From toddlers playing video games to teens navigating social media, it's more important than ever to stay on top of your kids' use of tech.

F rom toddlers to teens, kids today are more plugged in than ever. Research by Common Sense Media, a nonprofit group that focuses on how children interact with media and technology, found that children ages 8 and younger spend an average of 48 minutes a day staring at a mobile screen (that's three times the amount in 2013). And more than 42 percent of kids ages 8 and younger now have their own tablets.

By the time they've reached their teens, the vast majority (nearly 80 percent) of our kids have access to a smartphone–and you won't find them far from their devices most of the time. Common Sense Media reports

half of all teens feel addicted to their mobile devices, with 78 percent checking them at least hourly. For most, social media services like Instagram and Snapchat drive the need to constantly check in. Common Sense reports that 80 percent of teens and 23 percent of tweens have their own social media accounts.

As parents, most of us are also guilty of being tied to our devices. But researchers say that for kids, the consequences of being constantly wired can be far more damaging. "The prefrontal cortex of the brain is not complete until most people are in their mid to late 20s," explains Larry Rosen, PhD, professor emeritus in the psychology department at California State University,

Dominguez Hills and author of *The Distracted Mind: Ancient Brains in a High-Tech World.* This area of the brain plays a significant role in willpower, decision-making and the ability to think things through, says Rosen. Constantly scrolling through an Instagram feed or swiping through games may undermine the development of this crucial area of cognition. Other research has shown that the brains of young people diagnosed with internet addiction show significantly less gray matter, which is associated with planning, decision making and impulse control.

There are also other troubling signs when it comes to mental health. Some experts suspect that skyrocketing diagnoses of ADHD (up 43 percent between 2000 and 2010) may have everything to do with the amount of time kids spend in front of screens. "More kids today than ever before are struggling, and on some level these digital distractions may be to blame," says Thomas Kersting, a licensed psychotherapist and the author of *Disconnected: How to Reconnect Our Digitally Distracted Kids.* "Many kids today exhibit antisocial behaviors like struggling to make eye contact in conversation and difficulty forming friendships, along with poor coping skills." Some of this also occurs on a molecular level: There's a natural occurrence in adolescence called neural pruning, he says. "It's the brain's way of weeding out pathways that are used less often." If kids spend most of their time communicating through their devices and not face-to-face, the brain may weed out the neural pathways that are vital to becoming an in-person communicator, notes Kersting.

Other mental-health experts fear that social media and other technology may be contributing to higher rates of adolescent depression and suicide risk. The number of adolescents who experienced at least one major depressive episode was up 60 percent between 2010 and 2016, according to the U.S.

Department of Health and Human Services. And research shows 48 percent of teens who spend more than five hours a day on electronic devices report at least one suicide-related outcome (defined as: feeling very lonely and considering, planning or attempting suicide). Young women seem to be at the biggest risk–a report from the Centers for Disease Control and Prevention found that suicide rates among teen girls is at a 40-year high.

Technology can also affect kids in other ways. A 2014 study of 2-year-olds found that BMI increases for every hour per week of media consumption. And kids who watch more than two hours of TV daily have twice the risk of developing childhood obesity. A 2018 German study found that higher use of electronic media is linked to lower sleep quality in kids as young as age 3.

Of course, not all technology use is negative. Most of us find some relief in being able to constantly check in with our kids, whether it's figuring out how they're getting home from practice or reminding them of a doctor's appointment. And more than 40 percent of parents say media actually helps their children's relationships.

Still, given the many concerns we all have about our kids' use of technology, it helps to have an action plan in place. Not sure where to begin? Follow our expert tips for helping keep technology in your house under control.

✳ **Start young.**
"As soon as your child is using devices, you need to start talking about rules and what's right and wrong," says Nicole Beurkens, PhD, a licensed psychologist based in Grand Rapids, Michigan. Explain that tablets, phones and computers are not toys and should be handled with care. And talk about the importance of respecting privacy and protecting personal information in age-appropriate ways. "Our goal as parents is to be proactive, which means

It's not all bad: More than 40 percent of parents say technology actually helps their kids' relationships with their peers.

Have up-front and honest conversations with your kids about appropriate media use, including gaming.

thinking and talking about issues before they become a problem," Beurkens adds. Keep the conversation going, adding more information as your children get older.

* Emphasize safety.
"Kids need to know what information is safe to disclose," says Beurkens. That's especially true for younger children, who don't always set appropriate boundaries. "Explain what is appropriate to share and why there could be safety concerns." For older kids, emphasize the importance of not oversharing, posting inappropriate content, or being disrespectful in digital interactions. "Teach them that what they put out can't be taken back. Kids are growing up in a culture where boundaries are fluid, and they often don't understand the consequences of their actions," adds Beurkens.

* Establish limits.
"Parents have to monitor their children's use of technology. Period," says Rosen. The American Academy of Pediatrics (AAP) recommends zero screen-based media (except video chatting) for children under 18 months. For toddlers (18 to 24 months), the group advises parents should choose only "high-quality programming" and watch it alongside their child. The group advises children ages 2 to 5 have no more than one hour of high-quality programming a day, while those ages 6 and up have consistent limits on media. Rosen recommends kids under age 10 use technology for no more than 30 to 60 minutes a day; limit preteens (10 to 12) to about 60 to 90 minutes at a sitting; teens and adults, no more than 90 minutes at any one time before taking at least a 15- to 30-minute break.

* Ensure a no-phone zone.
We all need time away from our devices, says Rosen, who adds both adults and kids should have at least 1 to 2 hours a day with zero access to any devices. Create tech-free zones, like the dinner table and the bedroom, and use your time together to catch up. Just sitting down and having a talk with your child every day, even for just 15 minutes, can strengthen your relationship and assist in developing communication skills.

* Keep tech out of the bedroom.
The AAP reports that using digital media at night can interfere with sleep quality. Devices that emit blue light tend to hamper the body's production of melatonin, the hormone that controls the sleep-wake cycle, which can make it harder to fall asleep and stay asleep. According to the National Sleep Foundation, about 72 percent of children ages 6 to 17 sleep with at least one electronic device in the bedroom–which can lead to getting up to an hour's less sleep on school nights, compared with other kids. Put screens away at least 30 minutes before bedtime.

* Be a good role model.
Face it: You're probably on your device a lot more than you would like. In fact, according to Common Sense Media, parents spend more than nine hours a day on a screen. But 78 percent of all parents believe they are good technology role models for their children. The best way to model good behavior? Know when it's time to turn off your device. Whenever possible, leave your phone out of eyesight and focus on interacting with your child.

* Let your child get bored.
When you always have the world at your fingertips, there's no need for anyone to get bored. But that's not always a good thing, especially for kids. "Boredom is the Miracle-Gro for the mind and for your emotional well-being," says Kersting. "It's a form of mindfulness that we can all use to reflect and build creativity." When you're constantly

distracted by devices, your mind can't just roam free. "We have to teach our kids to embrace boredom, not avoid it," he adds.

✳ **Check in on what they're doing.**
A respect for privacy may be important, but parents still need to be aware of their kids' online activities, says Beurkens. About 40 percent of parents say they check the content of their children's devices and social media accounts always or most of the time. But while you can choose to incorporate parental controls, some experts say you are the best gatekeeper. Kids tend to get around parental controls anyway, and older kids tend to feel like their parents don't trust them. Continue to have up-front and honest conversations with your kids about healthy media use and remind them to think about what they are posting.

✳ **Use your tech together.**
Use some of your own screen time to get familiar with your kids' favorite games or service. Ask them to show you a favorite new game or check out the latest YouTube sensation. See what they're tuning in to, and show them some of your favorite (age-appropriate) stuff as well. It doesn't really matter if it's an educational video or a silly meme; it can just bring you closer.

Fight Tech Addiction

There are a few easy ways to make it easier to put the phone down— for a little while, at least.

Turn off notifications.
Every time your teen gets a ding that her latest post has been liked, it sends her straight to the app to start scrolling. Make it easier to ignore by turning off habit-forming push notifications.

Get rid of autoplay.
Services like Netflix, Facebook and YouTube keep an endless stream of videos on tap —so it's a lot harder to shut down. Reduce binge use by shutting off the default autoplay setting.

Break up streaks.
Apps like Snapchat encourage users to send posts for as many days as possible. If your child's streaks are turning into an obsession, limit use to once a day.

Get rid of in-app purchases.
Some popular games try to convince you to stay in the game by buying currency; they're also more likely to hit you up with other ads. Avoid the hassle by springing for the full, paid version.

Let's Talk About Sex

It's almost never too early to discuss the birds and the bees and offer up some straight insight on the subject.

When pediatrician Cora Breuner, MD, of Seattle Children's Hospital, talks about sex to a group of students ages 10 or 11 in an elementary school classroom, they aren't sheepish or bored. "I'm looking at 35 kids," she says, "and they're not looking away. They are rapt."

Breuner, a professor in the Department of Adolescent Medicine at the University of Washington and chair of the American Academy of Pediatrics Committee for Adolescence, doesn't bring up the details of sexual activity with this age group. Instead, she focuses on what they're wondering about most: how their bodies are changing– or likely soon will as puberty sets in. She talks to them about their growth spurts and about their anatomy. The specifics about the rest? That can come later.

Parents often dread the day when their child will ask where babies come from, and all too many put off frank conversations about sex altogether. But avoiding

Gender Identity and Sexual Orientation

Children become aware of their gender identity (how a person self-identifies) as young as 4 or 5 years old. Orientation (which sex a person is attracted to) usually begins around 8 years old.

While not every boy who wants to wear a dress is expressing gender in that way, parents need to be sensitive to the possible meaning of such behaviors.

For transgender children, the physical changes of puberty don't always match how they feel—and that can be distressing, so getting them support before the onset of puberty is important. A transgender child's safety at school can also be an issue, so find out about the school's policies toward their transgender students.

Parents likely won't know if their child is LGBQ (lesbian, gay, bisexual, queer) at first. By about second grade, children start to understand the idea of emotional relationships between adults and become curious about sexuality. Parents need to normalize different kinds of relationships before that time—such as discussing both same- and opposite-sex couples.

discussion of sex brings serious risk. "When it doesn't happen, we have unwanted pregnancies, sexually transmitted infections and misinformation about gender identity and fluidity," says Breuner. "It is much more difficult when we don't talk about it at all." Here's how to get the conversation going.

1 Start Soon

Some parents may think an elementary-school talk is way too soon to get the conversation about sex started. But "it's extremely important to understand that it's never too early to talk about this," says Breuner.

The key is to do more listening than talking while keeping the conversation age-appropriate. "A child asking at age 3 'Where do babies come from?' is very different from what they're asking at age 8, when the question is 'How does someone get pregnant?'" says Debra Hauser, president of Advocates for Youth, which focuses on sex education for teens. With the first question, the simple answer can be, "From their mothers." For the latter, the answer will involve a little more detail. The goal is to answer only the question they're asking, without digging too deep.

2 Spread It Out

Many parents attempt to have The Talk all in one go, in what Breuner calls an "information dump." But research suggests that when a parent dominates the conversation, teenagers come away with less knowledge. "You tend to want to jump in and offer all your thoughts" as a parent, adds Hauser. But sometimes kids just need a little more time to take it all in and ask questions of their own.

Kids' biggest questions about their sexuality tend to revolve around whether they are "normal."

3 Don't Dwell

The conversation doesn't have to last as long as you think it does. "It should be quick–a minute max," says Breuner. Stop when "you see your kid not paying attention anymore." Then return to the subject another time.

4 Find Teachable Moments

This can make the segue into talking about sexuality a little easier. "If there's something happening on screen while you're watching TV, bring up the conversation with your child," says Hauser. Parents can ask a child what they think about the relationship depicted, for example, or if they think a teen character who engaged in sex was old enough to do so. "These conversations kind of percolate up when the kids walk by the tampons in the store and ask, 'What's that for?'" she says. "You need to lodge that in your brain for later: 'I should talk about this–and not to death.'"

5 Play It Straight

Normalize whatever your child is asking about. "If you act shocked, you're going to shut them down," notes Hauser. The biggest thing most children want to know–at any age–is if they are "normal," she says. This need only intensifies as your child reaches puberty. "They're starting to get pubic hair or one breast is bigger than the other or they're attracted to someone of the same gender, and it's important to assure them that all kinds of thoughts and feelings are normal and real," adds Hauser.

6 Communicate as a Family

Some parents worry that talking about sex will encourage their children to try it too soon–but there's no evidence that is the case. And even if abstinence is the expectation for your child, it still requires discussion with him or her. Be sure to talk to your partner about what your expectations and rules are before discussing them with your children–and describe the consequences with your child upfront, says Breuner.

Should My Child Get the HPV Vaccine?

The human papillomavirus (HPV) is a virus that can cause venereal warts and throat, anal and cervical cancers. The HPV vaccine, which is administered in two shots, can prevent these issues, provided it is given early— before kids have been exposed to the virus. Kids who receive the vaccine series at the recommended age of between 9 and 11, before they become sexually active, mount a powerful immune response that lasts, Breuner says. Meanwhile, having the vaccinations later, even at age 15 or 16, yields a reduced response. And that could be too late: "It's way more difficult to protect kids once they become sexually active," explains Breuner.

7 Get Help if You Need It

Remember that sex education isn't only about anatomy and reproduction—it can also be about everything from relationships to gender identity to body image. Trusted online resources, such as the American Academy of Pediatrics (aap.org) or advocatesforyouth.org can provide some helpful material and guidelines about passing along age-appropriate information.

The Consent Conversation

One word has been entering the conversation about sex again and again recently, especially in light of the push for respect in the current age of #MeToo. That word is consent—the concept that no one may touch your body or have sex with you unless you actively agree. Consent is one of the earliest sex concepts children need to learn. Whether boy or girl, they must be able to both give and recognize consent—and teaching this takes more than a moment.

The consent concept is so important, says Hauser, that parents should always be laying the foundation for understanding what it means, almost from the time their children are born. That means teaching children the importance of respect for their own and others' boundaries and how to communicate their wishes to others.

Hauser gives the example of a neighbor seeing you with your toddler. If the neighbor says, "Oh, how cute! Come give me a hug," and your child clearly isn't comfortable with that, you should respect your child's reluctance. "Tell your child that it's OK [not to hug] and to come say hi instead," she explains.

The principles parents teach children about boundaries in nonsexual contexts can translate later. "You don't steal your brother's toy; you have to ask for permission to take it," Hauser notes, "and if he says no, you have to accept that answer." These childhood lessons are the beginnings of understanding and talking about consent.

Another important part of this ongoing learning process is using the correct names for body parts. Evidence shows that children who learn these terms by second grade have a reduced risk of being sexually abused. Knowing these terms also helps children articulate what they like and don't like. Modeling correct word use empowers children to use their communication skills to express their boundaries to others, adds Hauser.

THE BIG KID

MIDDLE CHILD

THE BABY

Establishing Order

Your children's birth order (oldest, middle, youngest)
can have a significant effect on their development.
Here's how to make sure everyone feels valued.

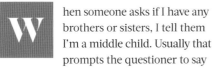

When someone asks if I have any brothers or sisters, I tell them I'm a middle child. Usually that prompts the questioner to say something along the lines of, "Oh, you must have middle-child syndrome," while laughing.

But in all this time, I never really knew what that was supposed to mean. It sounds like something negative–but how important is birth order, anyway? I asked some parenting experts just how much weight we should put on our kids' places in the family.

What's Middle-Child Syndrome, Anyway?

"Middle-child syndrome usually means the middle child has a specific kind of experience in the family, and that's how I look at all children in their birth order. A middle child often feels 'squeezed out,'" says Meri Wallace, LCSW, author of *Birth Order Blues: How Parents Can Help Their Children Meet the Challenges of Their Birth Order*, and a blogger for *Psychology Today*.

"A child who's clamoring for attention might be labeled as having 'middle-child syndrome,'" adds Wallace. "Often you may have an older sibling who is always doing new things and requires a lot of the family's attention, and you have the younger sibling who requires a lot of help and attention. The middle child often gets lost in the shuffle. When I wrote *Birth Order Blues*, I interviewed lots of kids and adults to learn their experiences. One little girl said to me, 'At nighttime, Dad is reading to my older brother, Mom is taking care of the baby, and I sit in the hallway on a chair and wait.'"

While I don't have any memories that specific about being "left out," I think I did try to keep the peace, follow the rules and bridge the relationship between my older sister and younger brother. My parents seemed nervous about everything my older sister did, probably because it was the first child doing something new, and I remember thinking that my younger brother got away with a lot more, and his punishments seemed more lenient when he acted up. But my parents did a good job of trying to balance their time with us. Both parents took me to sports practices and attended nearly every game as well as going to my school events, and they drove me to friends' houses and sleepovers.

"Family life is hard and complicated, because you have children sharing the resources, love and attention of the parents," says Wallace. "Whenever you have a situation of people sharing resources, it's difficult to make sure that everybody feels confident and equally loved."

But of course, as any parent knows, you can't be equally attentive to all your children, every minute. "You just want to try to make sure that each one has enough of you," says Wallace. "They need to feel that connection, because time equals attention, which equals love."

Parenting according to a child's order of birth can help parents be aware of what they could be doing more of. And that helps level the playing field a bit when it comes to making sure each child gets what he or she needs. Consider these typical characteristics of children born to different birth positions and how you can parent each child effectively.

Oldest Child

TYPICAL TRAITS

"The firstborn tends to be very bossy, has to make all the decisions, and must feel like he's No. 1," says Wallace. The oldest child is often a leader and might also feel more pressure to be perfect, she adds.

"When the second child is born, the oldest may exhibit some troublesome behavior, because they're feeling displaced by a younger sibling," explains Wallace. "This happens to every firstborn. At some point, they're 'dethroned.' They were once No. 1– and now they're not."

PARENTING TIPS

Encourage your oldest to speak up about any feelings of anger or jealousy he may have about his sibling(s), advises Wallace. "These emotions are normal, and voicing them is better than keeping them bottled up inside." Since your firstborn is more likely to feel pressured to be perfect, make a special effort

X

Firstborns tend to be bossy; middle children more accommodating; and last-borns more rebellious and outgoing.

Oldest, middle, youngest? Give each of them a chance to practice leadership skills and make decisions.

A 2009 study found birth order influences who we choose as friends and spouses, often associating with those who have a similar birth position.

to assure him that he has your unconditional love, she says. "Reassure your oldest that you have enough love for her and your new baby." Make an effort to spend some one-on-one time with your eldest once the second or third child arrives. "Allow the firstborn time to play with their peers without their siblings interrupting their space."

Middle Child

TYPICAL TRAITS

"The second-born child tends to be more flexible than her older sibling," explains Wallace. "They have an older sibling who wants to go first all the time, and [the second child] wants to be included. The second child is often a pleaser and wants to make sure that the older one likes him." The middle child is more flexible and will often let the older one go first to keep her happy so they can play together. Middle children also tend to be extremely competitive with their siblings and need to establish their own unique identity, since they are neither the oldest nor youngest.

As a middle child, I tend to think of myself as pretty easygoing. I would rather keep the peace and have everyone enjoying themselves than to "win" at something. I'm fortunate that my older sister never seemed to mind me following her and her friends around. (I, on the other hand, was more annoyed by my little brother following my friends and me around.)

Wallace's statement about establishing "my own unique identity" holds true with me. After college, I moved to New York City, focused on my career, went on exciting trips

and adventures and established myself as a writer. My siblings stayed closer to home–and while perhaps I thought this adventurous spirit "was just me," it might have to do more with my birth order.

PARENTING TIPS

Try letting your second-born go first once in a while–they need that experience, says Wallace. "This will help give them leadership skills that they'll need in the future," she notes. Since the second-born is often rushing to catch up to the firstborn, it's important for parents to praise the second child's abilities and celebrate his successes, even if when he wins the spelling bee or soccer championship it's the second time around for the family.

"Encourage this child's interests so they develop their unique sense of self," says Wallace. The second-born might want to do everything the older sibling does, but take the time to explore their talents–like an artistic skill–and encourage those, even if the older child didn't take drawing classes. Remind the middle child that they can't do everything their older sibling is participating in right now because of their age gap–and that this is OK.

Youngest Child

TYPICAL TRAITS

Last-borns tend to be more rebellious and outgoing; they don't feel the perfectionist pressure firstborns may experience. According to psychologist Kevin Leman, PhD, in *The Birth Order Book: Why You Are the Way You Are*, the youngest are often "uncomplicated, spontaneous, humorous and high in people skills. To them, life's a party. They're most likely to get away with murder and least likely to be punished." (Maybe that's why so many famous comics tend to be last-borns?)

I grew up thinking my younger brother got a lot of my parents' attention and wasn't sure if that was because he was the baby or the boy. Perhaps that was my perception as the middle child. But my fiancé–a last-born–fits the description of being funny, outgoing and social, with a rebellious streak.

PARENTING TIPS

Leman says the youngest often gets picked on and is more likely to get hand-me-downs than the older siblings. The parent should be conscious of this and make sure the youngest still gets new things that they own first, while creating their own sense of identity.

"Be on the lookout for older siblings picking on the youngest one, and make sure the baby gets to be first during activities and practice his or her leadership skills as well," advises Wallace. Make sure they're still being given chores–like filling up the dog's water bowl or cleaning up their toys–so they have a sense of responsibility, even if they are small.

The baby of the family can sometimes be ignored and left to themselves, or they can be more likely to be mischievous and attention-seeking–oftentimes in the form of being entertaining, writes Leman. Even if the last-born seems like he or she is doing just fine on their own, make sure you're giving them attention and are aware of what they're getting into. It's a good way to make sure everyone in your family feels secure and happy.

–Diana Kelly Levey

Giving your children free time to play and bond keeps relationships strong for life.

Life Lessons

Grandparents have much to offer to younger generations.
Encourage them to share their wisdom and experience.

G randparents are in a unique position when it comes to teaching kids about what really matters in life. Not only do they have a boatload of hard-won wisdom bobbing at the surface, but the stories about their lives can maximize a child's understanding of the world. "Grandparents play such a crucial role in helping kids see beyond the here and now," notes Ana Homayoun, educator, school consultant and author of *Social Media Wellness: Helping Tweens and Teens Thrive in an Unbalanced Digital World.* "By sharing their life

experiences, grandparents are able to help kids develop a sense of perspective that there are ebbs and flows in life." For example, a child may be deeply disappointed by not making the baseball team or getting a part in the school play. "A grandparent can share his or her life perspective on a time something didn't go as planned, and what positive forces bloomed out of that disappointment," adds Homayoun. "They can help them realize that setbacks, while disappointing, don't necessarily halt things from moving on."

In addition to teaching kids perseverance, grandparents are integral in giving children a sense of identity and confidence, researchers have found. In fact, they may be the ultimate influencers when it comes to matters of human character.

Kindness

The Golden Rule that we learned back in the day remains a valuable mantra: "Do unto others as you would have them do unto you." In today's world, with kids surrounded by a me-first attitude perpetuated by everything from reality TV to cutthroat politics, teaching them compassion and to think about more than themselves is more important than ever. "Despite all these outside forces, kids get much of their modeling from those they come into contact with on a regular basis, including grandparents," says Homayoun, who writes about "cele-bratty" culture in her book *The Myth of the Perfect Girl*. "Grandparents who are able to have active conversations with their grandchildren, and ask open-ended questions without judgment, can really make the concept of kindness and respect come alive for kids." If something on TV or online seems uncivil or mean, it could be an opportunity for a nonjudgmental conversation: What did you think? What would you have done differently? What might a kinder approach have been?

Generosity

Selflessness is a quality often learned by example, so be aware that an adult's behavior toward others will set the bar for little eyes and ears. Journalist Marisa Hillman recalls the lasting impression her grandmother made with her unceasing altruism: "I can't think of a single time when [she] put herself first," Hillman has noted. "Even at the very end, she was the one comforting *me* when it finally sunk in that she was dying. She spent her life working as a nurse and enjoyed caring for others; she

Teaching kindness and compassion from a very young age can help grandchildren grow into concerned, caring adults.

Most children
want to be helpful
and to be of
service to others.

said it was fulfilling. And, of course, she was right. And, of course, she was right. We're all in this crazy life together, so let's take care of each other."

Love and Relationships

Every grandparent has his or her own experience in terms of relationships, and kids can benefit from their wisdom and perspective, whether it's to choose a partner with similar goals, marry your best friend, or make compromise easy. As for the value of building strong friendships, seeing is, again, believing. "For grandparents who have deep networks and meaningful friendships, it's beneficial for kids to see how those relationships are nurtured over time," says Homayoun. "Many of our daily experiences have become transactional in nature. Try bringing a grandchild along to visit a sick friend, deliver a birthday cake or give a friend a ride to the airport."

Work Ethic

All kids have dreams, but not all understand that they must work for their dreams– that just believing in them is not enough. Encouraging a healthy work ethic early on will serve a child for years to come. Grandparents can encourage kids to pitch in and be helpful by "allowing them to shine and contribute in ways that make them feel useful," suggests Homayoun. "Letting children be part of something greater than themselves–say, by taking on tasks for a dinner or helping to plan a trip–gives them a sense of autonomy and offers them a feeling of competence. It also promotes a sense of community and belonging." While assigning chores may seem like a good lesson in hard work, the word "chore" can be off-putting, implying something is a "chore" to do. Chores may also be counterproductive in helping kids develop an intrinsic motivation. A better approach may be creating opportunities for kids to use or develop skills that contribute to a larger project, be it with family, school or community.

Money and Business

Ashby Daniels, a financial planner in Pittsburgh, credits his grandfather with sparking his interest in the business world. "He showed me how to track stocks in the newspaper and how they worked," he says. "Even into his 70s and 80s, he continued to educate himself, which was not lost on me. Seeing him read the business section to glean insights made me strive to get better each day." While different grandparents have varying financial means, all can instill the concept that making money feels as good as spending it. As for managing money, "it's a good idea to start with the concept of save, spend, share," says Homayoun. "With every dollar earned, encourage kids to decide what percentage they will save, how much they are able to spend and what can be shared with others. Talking with kids about how and where they would share their money can be empowering as well." As for learning to live within a budget, ask a grandparent to take your kids shopping with a gift card. Because they can't spend over the amount on the card, they'll learn how to choose wisely within a certain dollar range.

Resilience

Helping kids develop buoyancy–reducing the time and energy it takes them to bounce back from a disappointment–is a valuable survival skill that lends itself well to a grandparent's life experiences. Grandparents can share about a time when they got stuck and were mired down, then how they found a path forward. "It isn't about lessening pain or overlooking grief," notes Homayoun. "It's about giving kids the time and space needed to process and move on by thinking about opportunities with a focus on self-compassion and self-care."

Regardless of how much money you have, grandkids benefit most from your time.

INDEX

CREDITS

COVER Flashpop/Getty Images FRONT FLAP Flashpop/Getty Images 2-3 Flashpop/ Getty Images 4 Jose Luis Pelaez Inc/Getty Images 6-7 wundervisuals/Getty Images 8-11 Geber86/Getty Images (2) 14 Sam Edwards/Getty Images 17 Mike Kemp/Getty Images 20 PeopleImages/Getty Images 22-23 Johner RF/Getty Images 26 wundervisuals/Getty Images 28-29 Michael H/Getty Images 31 Clarissa Leahy/Getty Images 32 ImaZinS RF/ Getty Images 35 B. Boissonnet/Getty Images 37 Christina Kennedy/Getty Images 38 Juice Images/Getty Images 41 damircudic/Getty Images 43 Taiyou Nomachi/Getty Images 44-45 Zia Soleil/Getty Images 46 Jose Luis Pelaez Inc/Getty Images 49 Westend61/Getty Images 52 Tetra Images/Getty Images 54-55 images by Tang Ming Tung/Getty Images 58 Sergey Novikov/Shutterstock 61 Jose Luis Pelaez Inc/Getty Images 62-63 Erik Isakson/Getty Images 65 10'000 Hours/Gary Burchell/Getty Images 66 Carol Yepes/Getty Images 68-69 Paul Bradbury/Getty Images 72 SensorSpot/Getty Images 75 Image Source/Getty Images 77 UrsaHoogle/Getty Images 78 BraunS/Getty Images 81 patrickheagney/Getty Images 83 moodboard/Getty Images 84 Geber86/Getty Images 86-87 franckreporter/Getty Images 89 skynesher/Getty Images 90 Betsie Van der Meer/Getty Images 92-93 kali9/Getty Images 94 JGI/Jamie Grill/Tetra images RF/Getty Images 96-97 SDI Productions/Getty Images 99 Emely/Cultura RF/Getty Images 100-101 Choreograph/Getty Images 102 Petri Oeschger/Getty Images 105 Alexandra Grablewski/Getty Images 106-107 kate_sept2004/ Getty Images 108-109 Mikolette/Getty Images 110 PIKSEL/Getty Images 113 Comstock Images/Getty Images 115 FatCamera/Getty Images 116 Mike Kemp/Tetra images RF/Getty Images 118-119 Portra Images/Getty Images 121 SDI Productions/Getty Images 122-123 Digital Vision./Getty Images 124 SolStock/Getty Images 126-127 PeopleImages/Getty Images 131 Alena Ozerova/Shutterstock 134-135 FilippoBacci/Getty Images 139 Image Source/Getty Images 141 JGI/Jamie Grill/Getty Images 142-143 Dreet Production/MITO images/Getty Images 144 Tetra Images/Getty Images 146 JGI/Jamie Grill/Getty Images 148 Wilaipon Pasawat/EyeEm/Getty Images 150 American Images Inc/Getty Images 152-153 PeopleImages/Getty Images 156 Carol Yepes/Getty Images 158-159 Linda Raymond/Getty Images 162 Tony Tallec/Alamy Stock Photo 165 Paul Bradbury/Getty Images 168 Digital Vision./Getty Images 170-171 Martin Dimitrov/Getty Images 173 Westend61/Getty Images 174 Vladimir Godnik/fStop/Getty Images 177 Imgorthand/Getty Images 179 Darrin Klimek/ Getty Images 180-185 Jose Luis Pelaez Inc/Getty Images (3) BACK FLAP Flashpop/Getty Images BACK COVER Symphonie Ltd/Getty Images

Special thanks to contributing writers:

Lindsey Emery, Diana Kelly Levey, Joanna Powell, Andrea Pyros,
Brittany Risher, Katherine Schreiber, Celia Shatzman, Deborah Skolnik,
Michelle Stacey, Emily Willingham

CENTENNIAL BOOKS

An Imprint of
Centennial Media, LLC
40 Worth St., 10th Floor
New York, NY 10013, U.S.A.

CENTENNIAL BOOKS is a trademark of Centennial Media, LLC

All rights reserved. No part of this publication may be reproduced, stored in a retrieval system, or transmitted in any form or by any means (including electronic, mechanical, photocopying, recording, or otherwise) without prior written permission from the publisher.

ISBN 978-1-951274-28-3

Distributed by
Simon & Schuster, Inc.
1230 Avenue of the Americas
New York, NY 10020, U.S.A.

For information about custom editions, special sales and premium and corporate purchases, please contact Centennial Media at contact@centennialmedia.com.

Manufactured in China

© 2020 by Centennial Media, LLC

Publishers & Co-Founders Ben Harris, Sebastian Raatz
Editorial Director Annabel Vered
Creative Director Jessica Power
Executive Editor Janet Giovanelli
Deputy Editors Ron Kelly, Alyssa Shaffer
Design Director Ben Margherita
Art Director Andrea Lukeman
Art Directors Natali Suasnavas, Joseph Ulatowski
Assistant Art Director Jaclyn Loney
Photo Editor Kim Kuhn
Production Manager Paul Rodina
Production Assistant Alyssa Swiderski
Editorial Assistant Tiana Schippa
Sales & Marketing Jeremy Nurnberg